THE P·I·N·C·U·S·H·I·O·N BOOK

WORKBOX ENTERPRISES LIMITED
40 Silver Street, Wiveliscombe, Taunton, Somerset, TA4 2NY.

Typesetting & Origination: MR Reprographics, Chard, Somerset
Printers: A Wheaton & Co. Ltd., Exeter
Photography: Jona Sparey
Stitch Illustrations: Coats Leisure Craft Group

ISBN 0 9516825 0 4

Contents

CHARACTERS

NOVELTY

MISCELLANEOUS

Introduction

All the pincushions in this book were made by readers of "Workbox" needlecraft magazine. They are a varied and fascinating mixture of shapes, sizes and techniques, so you are sure to enjoy many happy hours making your own personal favourites. The delightful illustrations will also stimulate further ideas, as nearly all the pincushions offer scope for variations and adaptations.

Making a selection of the pincushions to be included in this book was quite a difficult task, but was ultimately decided by how well they photographed. If the photograph didn't look appealing, then it was, regretfully, not chosen. However, all the pincushions will be on permanent display at National Needle Museum, Redditch, Worcestershire, so you will have the opportunity to see them there.

C·A·N·V·A·S W·O·R·K

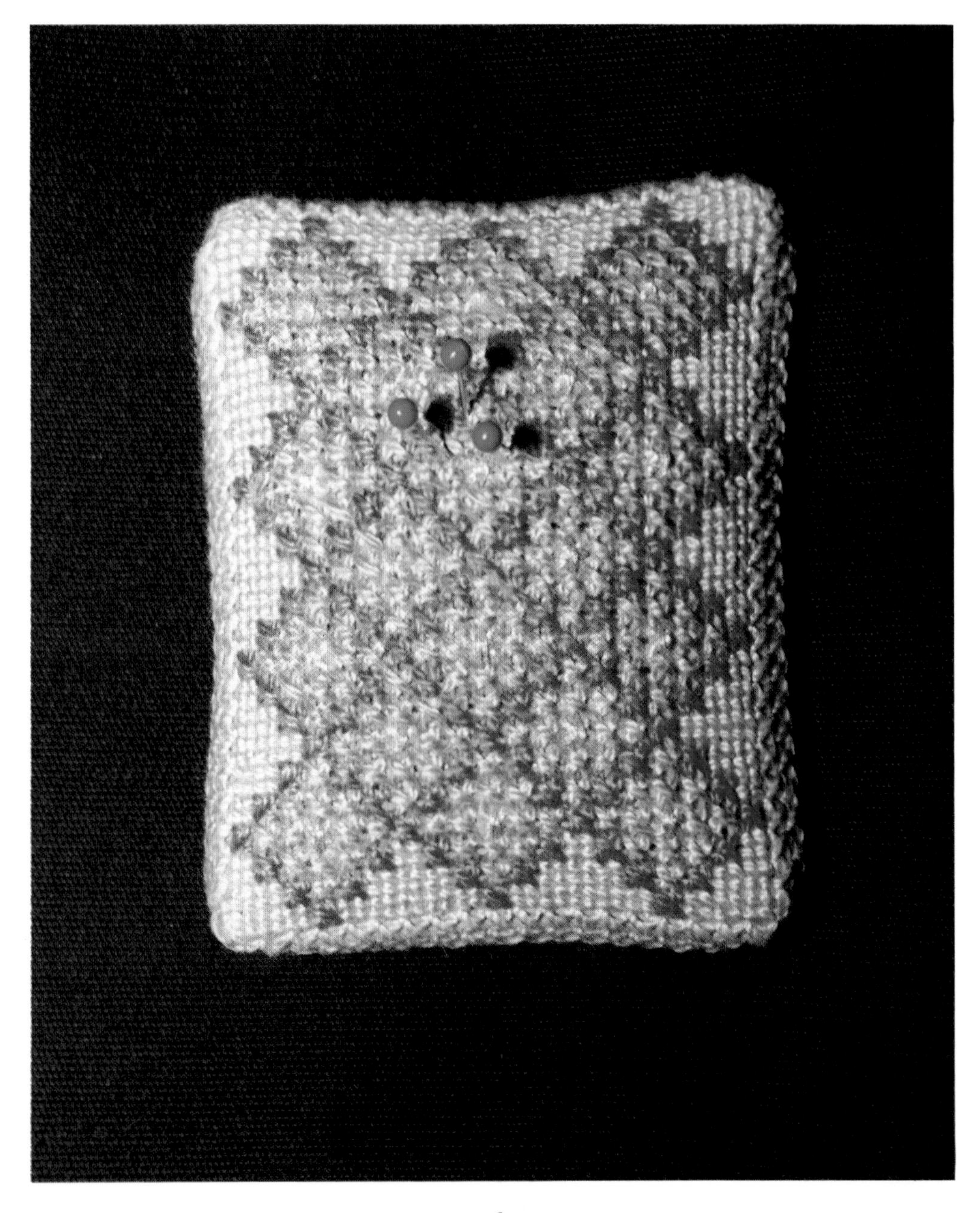

Blue Trellis

Materials
6 square inches of best quality canvas, 14 holes to the inch.
Three contrasting colours of D.M.C. Coton perle size 5.
1 yard lurex thread - silver or gold (optional)

Method
1 Work 25 squares in cross stitch.

2 Work tent stitch over one thread to edge.

3 Leaving corners unworked, work 3 rows of long-armed cross stitch.

4 Backstitch over 2 threads at base.

5 Cut a piece of stiff card same size as top of work.

6 Stick a piece of fabric over this.

7 Turn unworked corners towards each other and join.

8 Stuff pin cushion with wool or wadding.

9 Stitch base firmly to base of pin cushion.

(Cynthia Kendzior)

Long-Armed Cross Stitch

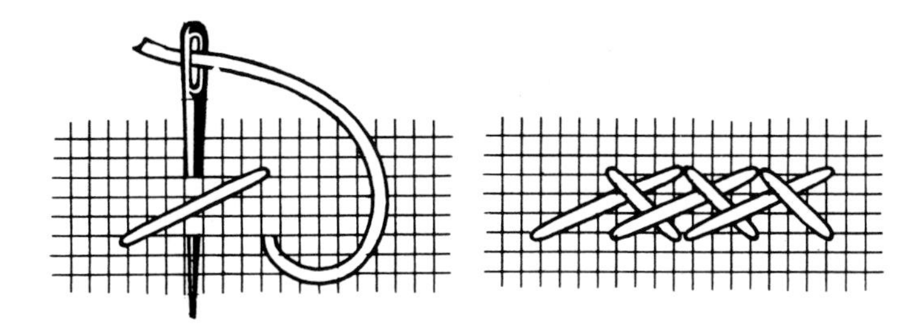

Canvas Work Tile

Materials
6 square inches of best quality canvas, 14 holes to the inch
5 contrasting colours of D.M.C. coton perle No. 5
16 small gold beads and beading needle (optional)
One length of 'gold finger' thread

Method
1 Large centre square consists of 24 squares, alternate tent and cushion stitch of 16 thread each with 16 beads in centre.

2 2 rows all round of tent stitch.

3 1 row slanting stitch over and across 2 threads.

4 1 row slanting stitch over and across in the opposite direction.

5 Back stitch of lurex thread between these two rows.

6 4 rows of tent stitch all round.

7 Finish top with long armed cross stitch over 2 threads all round.

8 Leaving corners unworked, stitch 3 rows of long-armed cross stitch ending with back stitch over 3 threads.

9 Join corners together.

10 Cut a piece of card the same size as top of work and stick a piece of fabric over this.

11 Stuff cushion with wool or wadding.

12 Stitch base firmly to base of cushion.

(Cynthia Kendzior)

Sequinned Trellis

Materials
6 square inches of best quality canvas, 14 holes to the inch
Two contrasting colours of D.M.C. Coton perle size 5
25 cup shaped sequins, 25 small matching beads

Method
1 Work 25 squares in cross stitch.

2 Work tent stitch over one thread to edge.

3 Leaving corners unworked, do 3 rows of long armed cross stitch.

4 Backstitch over 2 threads at base.

5 Sew sequins on in a pattern.

6 Cut a piece of stiff card the same size as top of work.

7 Stick a piece of fabric over this.

8 Turn unworked corners towards each other and join.

9 Stuff pin cushion with wool or wadding.

10 Stitch base firmly to base of pincushion.

(Cynthia Kendzior)

Florentine

(An original four-way Florentine design)

Materials

A 7 inch square of tapestry canvas, twenty threads per inch
A number 24 Tapestry needle
Masking tape
D.M.C. Medicis wool - Numbers: 8403, 8324, 8412A, 8304, 8401, 8303, 8419, 8327, 8420, 8328
A piece of linen for backing, 5½ins stuffing square

Method

1 Cover raw edges of canvas with masking tape to avoid wool catching.

2 Embroider, using two strands of thread, and weave ends in to start and finish off. To start, count 26 threads down from top edge of canvas and 32 threads in from right hand edge. Where these lines cross near the right hand corner is the point to bring your needle up from the back of the work. Using the chart to follow both colour scheme and stitch length, work each row as a complete round before going on to the next colour. The centre motif is worked in tent stitch.

3 Trim canvas to ⅝" all round tapestry. With right sides together, stitch linen backing to canvas keeping machine line as close to tapestry as possible. Leave a gap along one edge to allow for turning inside out. Trim seams and corners, turn, stuff and slip stitch open seams together.

4 Make a length of twisted cord from one of the colours used in the design and neatly stitch along outside edge. Finish with tassles at corners if desired.

(Elizabeth Winter)

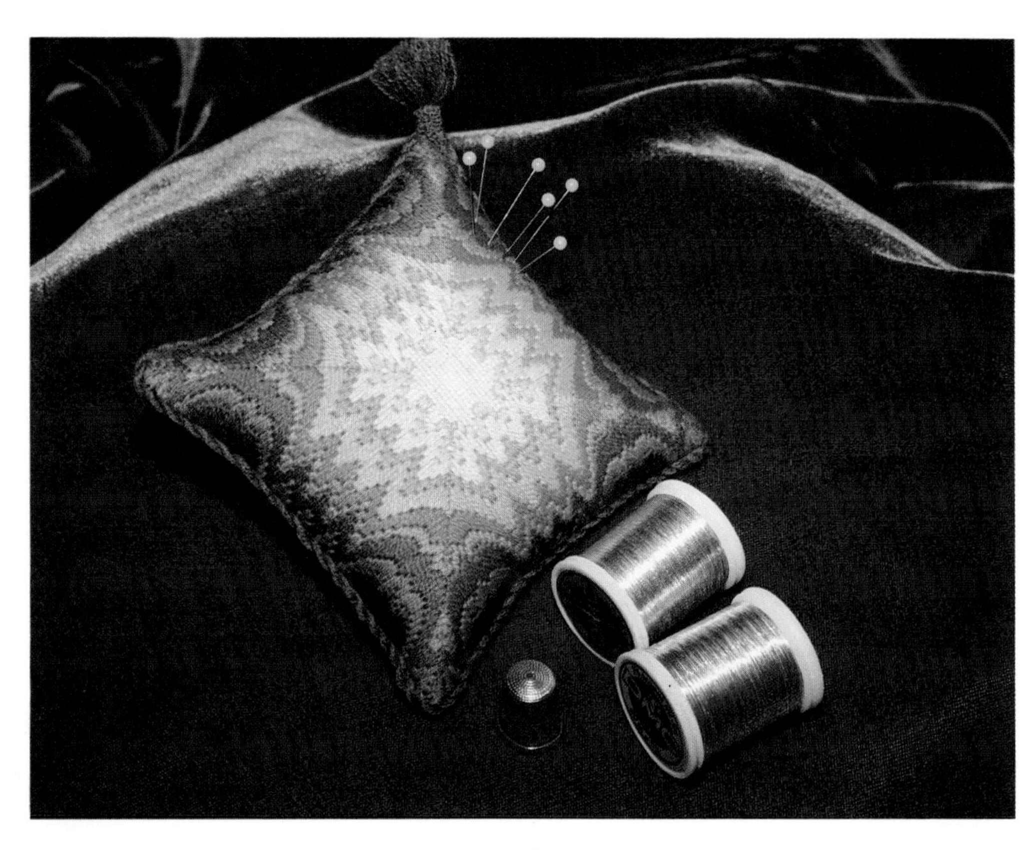

The chart shows only one quarter of the finished design. Work from right to left, turn canvas clockwise then copy design again, repeat until a square is formed.

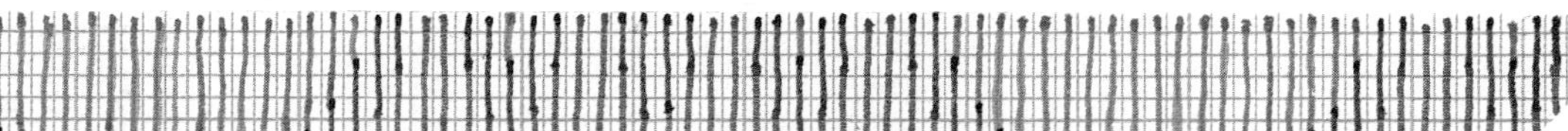

= 8403	= 8304	= 8419
= 8324	= 8401	= 8327
= 8412A	= 8303	= 8420

Colour 8328 is used for **centre tent stitch** motif.

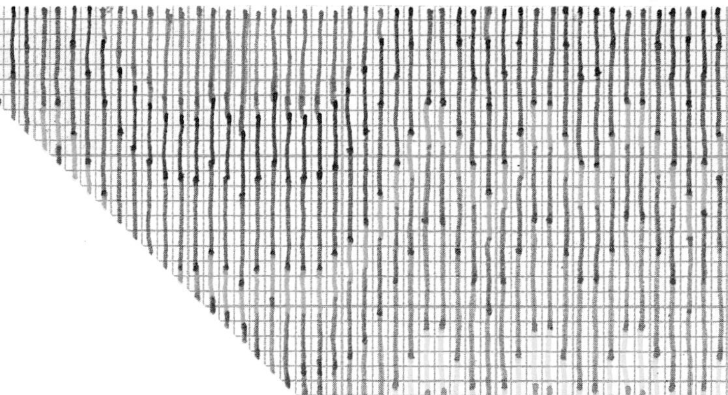

Mosaic

Materials
Piece of 16 count canvas 13 cms square (5 inches)
Oddments of 3 or 4 ply Knitting Wool
Piece of velvet the same size as the canvas
Small quantity of filling

Method
1 Follow the chart, leaving about half an inch canvas margin all round for turnings. If thicker wool than 3 or 4 ply is used, gently ease out 1 ply and discard it, this will give you the correct thickness for the canvas. The chart is made out for brown and orange colouring, but it looks equally attractive made up in blues and greens, or pinks and mauves.

2 When the canvas work is finished, place the right side of work and right side of velvet together, double tack, as the velvet 'creeps' a bit.

3 Then backstitch all around leaving a small gap for filling. Trim off unwanted canvas and velvet, turn right side out.

4 Fill the cushion until it is firm, and then oversew the gap together.

5 Make a small tassel for each corner with a strand of all colours used on the canvas.

(Joyce Routledge)

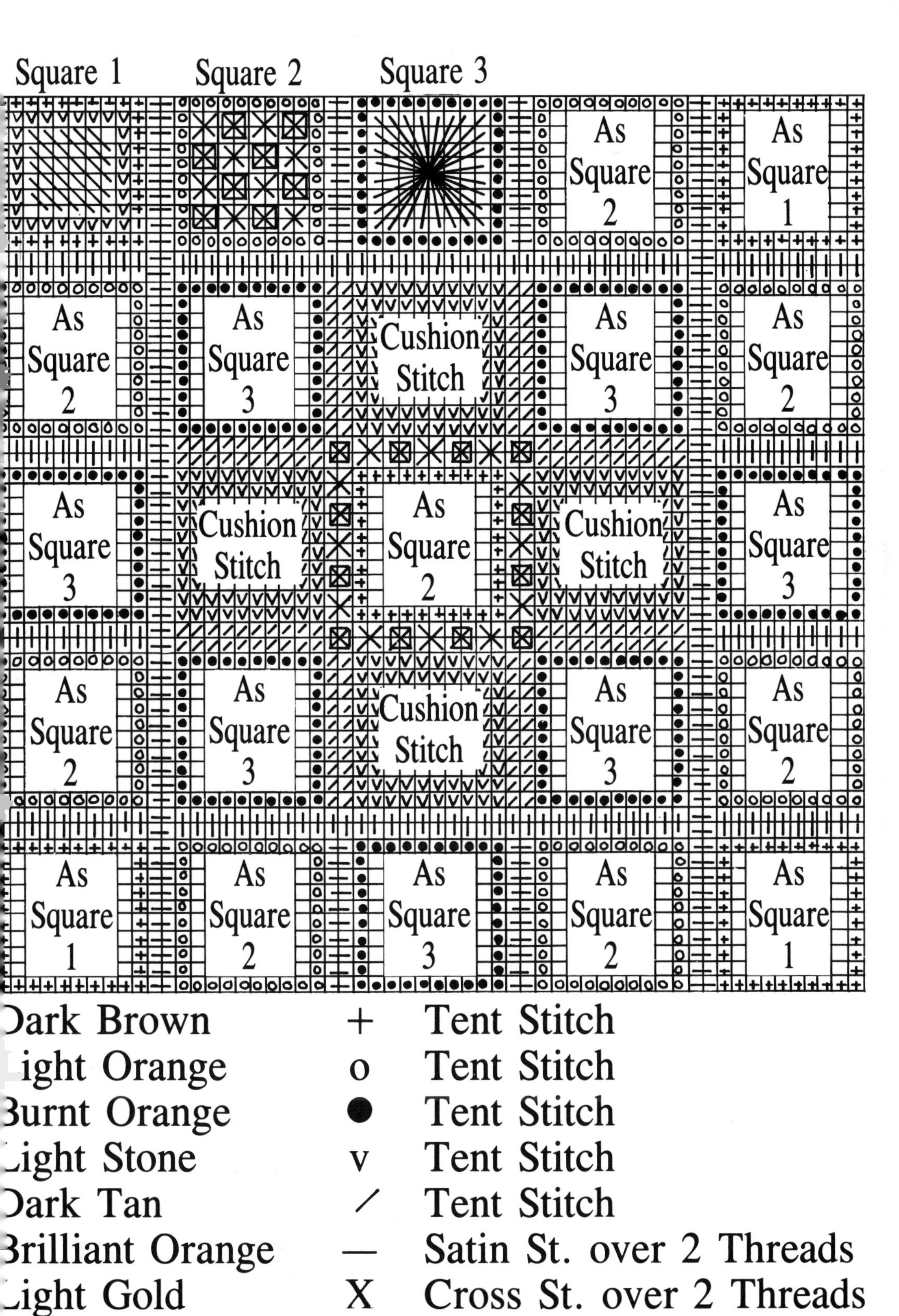
Square 1
Square 2
Square 3
As Square 2
As Square 1
As Square 2
As Square 3
Cushion Stitch
As Square 3
As Square 2
As Square 3
Cushion Stitch
As Square 2
Cushion Stitch
As Square 3
As Square 2
As Square 3
Cushion Stitch
As Square 3
As Square 2
As Square 1
As Square 2
As Square 3
As Square 2
As Square 1
ark Brown + Tent Stitch
ight Orange o Tent Stitch
urnt Orange ● Tent Stitch
ight Stone v Tent Stitch
ark Tan / Tent Stitch
rilliant Orange — Satin St. over 2 Threads
ight Gold X Cross St. over 2 Threads
ark Gold X Cross St. over 2 Threads

Katie's "Leftover" Pincushion

Whenever my Grandmother did a piece of embroidery, whether it was for herself or as a gift, she used to keep all of her leftover threads together in a little purse which she had bought on holiday in Venice. When her embroidery was finished she would get out the purse and a piece of evenweave linen and make one of her 'leftover' pin cushions which would accompany the piece of embroidery she had completed. All of the pin cushions were different sizes and designs, but they were all in cross stitch.

I have continued the tradition which my grandmother started and the samplers which I make for people as gifts are always accompanied by one of 'Katie's leftover pin cushions' which remind me of her and also appeal to the thrifty side of my nature, as I would hate to throw good embroidery thread away.

The pin cushion which I have made here is a simple spiral design which gives a log-cabin like effect, but you can have fun making your own designs with stripes of colour, both straight and diagonal, or checks of four cross stitches; once you start to think about it the possibilities are endless.

P.S. I hope you will forgive the late arrival of my pin cushion. I've only just heard about the competition from a friend who thought that I already knew. I hope you will accept it as I sat up until 12.30 last night making it and got up at 7 this morning to write the instructions, (a job which was far more difficult than I anticipated!)

Materials

6″ square of any evenweave material
5″ embroidery hoop - optional
Tapestry needle which will travel through the holes in the fabric without disturbing the weave of the cloth
Leftover lengths of stranded cotton
Calico or similar material for backing
Stuffing

Method

1 Take the piece of material and stretch it on the embroidery hoop if you like to use one.

2 Using 3 strands of cotton start your first cross in the centre of the hoop. Each cross is worked individually (over 2 threads in the case of material like hardanger or evenweave linen but over 1 box on material like Aida). Work around the first cross stitch in a spiral design. Keep going until you have used up all of your thread or you have reached the size you want. (The one in the illustration is 2 inches square).

3 Take the material off the frame and press.

4 Put a piece of calico behind the embroidery which will prevent the stuffing from coming up through the holes in the material. Put another piece of calico over the right side of the embroidery so that it is sandwiched between the two.

5 Sew around the edge of the embroidery either with a sewing machine or using back-stitch if sewing by hand. Leave a small opening on one side.

6 Turn the work the correct way out and stuff the cushion with the filling you have chosen.

7 Slip stitch the opening together.

Note: If the cushion you have made is large you may wish to make a tassel out of the leftover thread and sew it onto one corner of the cushion so that you can lift it up without being pricked, but I don't think that this is necessary on a small cushion.

(Susan Hopson)

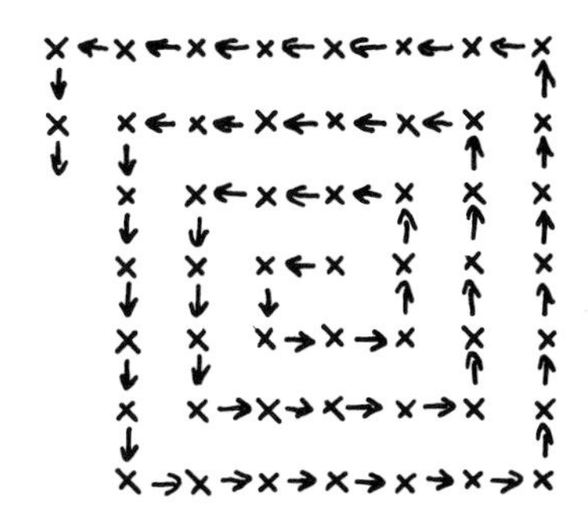

"Pins 'N Needles"

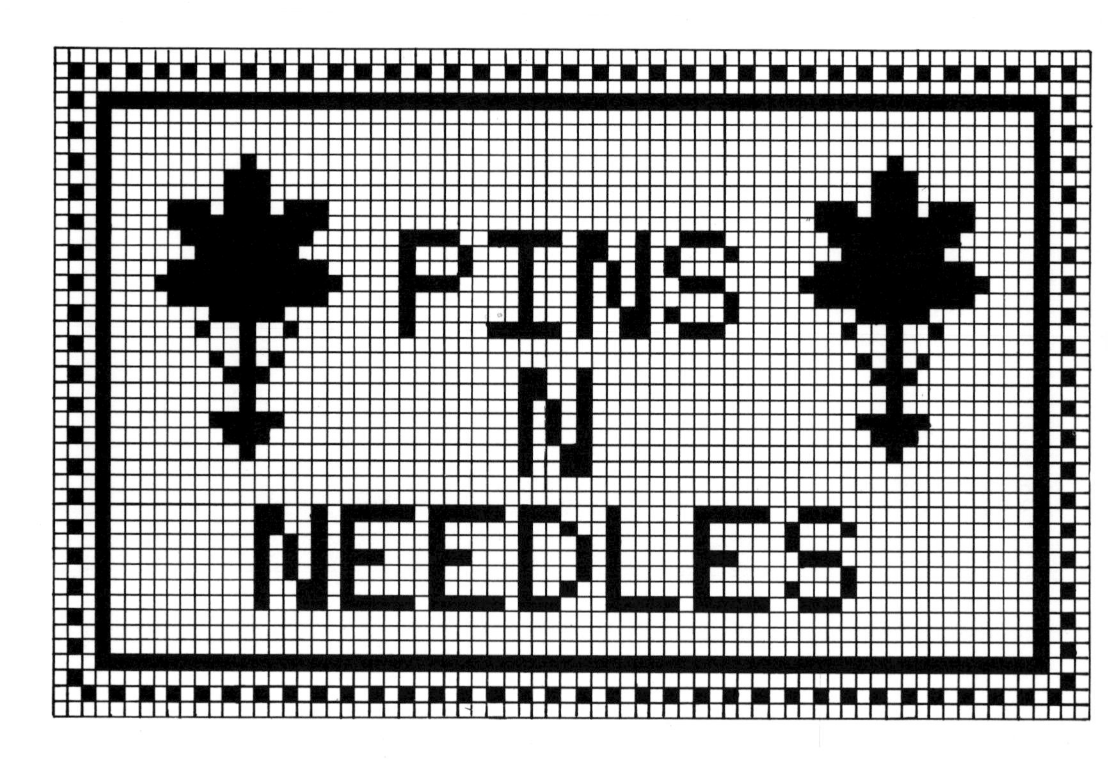

Materials
Double thread canvas 6 x 8 ins. (15 x 20 cm)
Backing fabric (15 x 20 cms)
Skein of embroidery thread: Pink, Green, Mauve, Beige, Blue, Yellow and White.
Foam for stuffing.

Method
1 Working in cross stitch, and using three strands, follow the graph pattern, referring to the photographs for colours.
NB. Start stitching from the centre of the design and your fabric.

2 Make up the pin cushion by sewing the embroidered top to the backing fabric, right sides together, on three sides. Use a neat back stitch.

3 Trim seam to 1 cm, cut off corners, then turn to right side.

4 Carefully push out corners, using scissors, then stuff with foam filling.

5 Stitch up the opening firmly and neatly.

(Sharon Sayers)

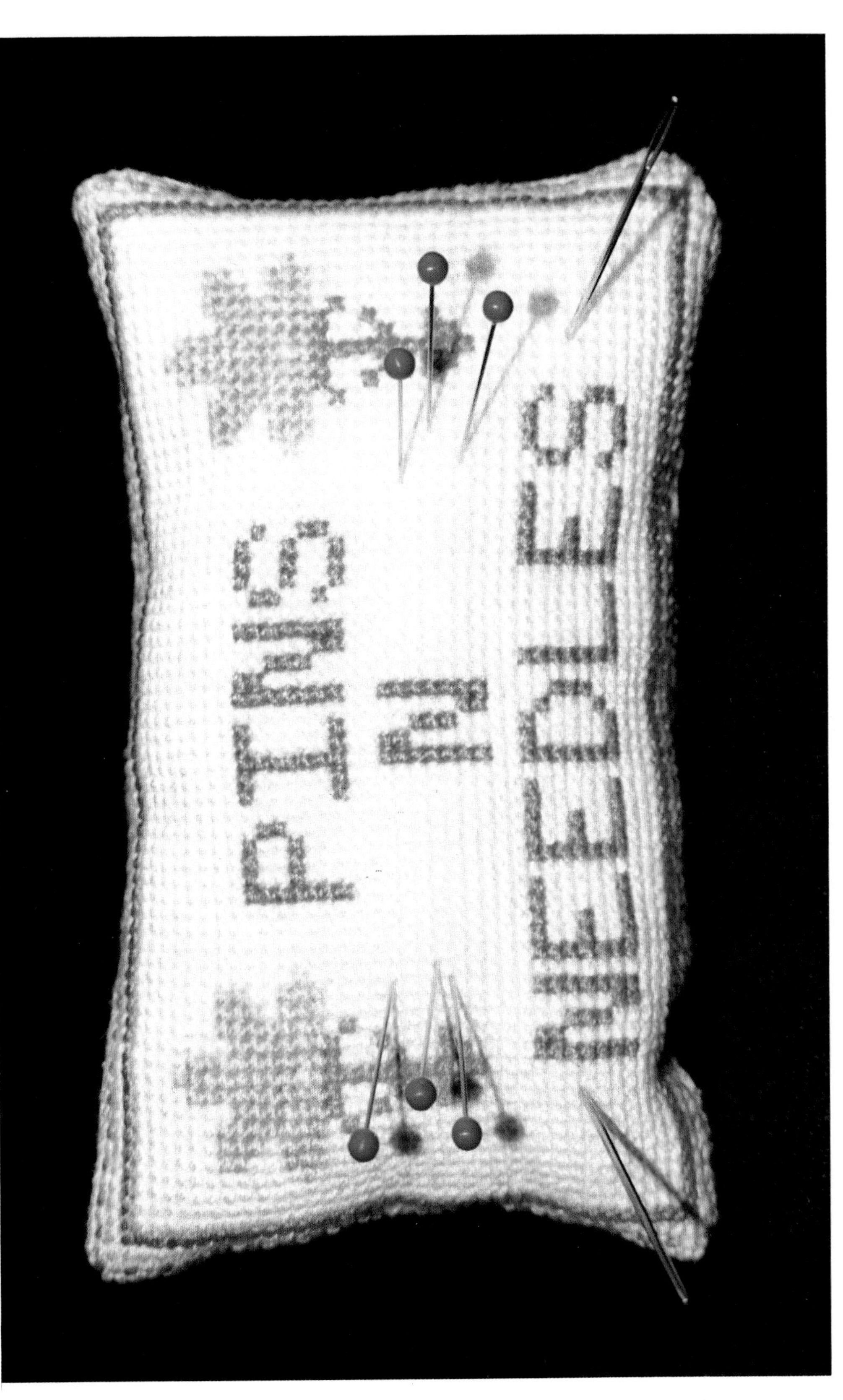
PINS
N
NEEDLES

Christmas Cushion

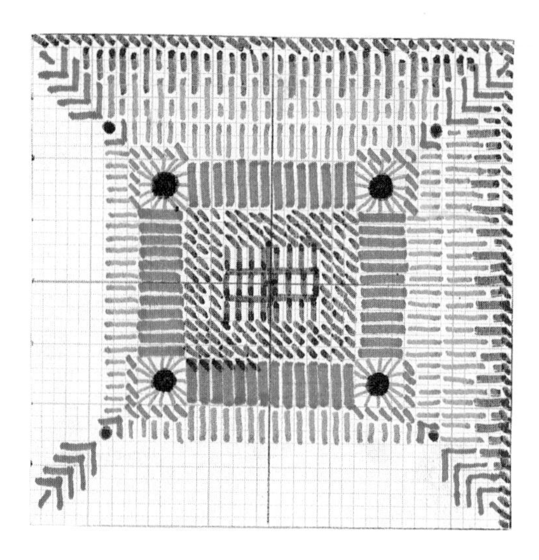

Materials
Interlock canvas 2/10th cm gauge
Red or green velvet for backing
Tapestry needle (size 18)
Different shades of GREEN wools - dark, medium and pale
RED wool

Method

1 Using red wool work 3 rows Gobelin straight stitch over two threads of canvas in the centre, to form a rectangle.

2 With the same colour, work three rows of Tent stitch round the rectangle.

3 Using dark green wool, work Gobelin straight stitch over FOUR threads, leaving the corners free.

4 Fill the corners with Algerian eye stitch, using pale green wool.

5 Using red wool, work a French knot over the Algerian eye stitch.

6 Using dark green wool, work Tent stitch over one thread on two corners only (next to French knots).

7 Using medium green wool, work round in straight Gobelin stitch, varying the length, to form an even square.

8 Using pale green, work round again, in long and short stitch (over two and four threads).

9 Using dark green, fill in corners, with two stitches.

10 Using red wool, work a row of tent stitch, filling spaces.

11 Using dark green, work each corner in straight stitches, at an angle.

12 Using red wool, work a row of long and short stitches, over two and four threads.

13 Turn over the edges and work a row of tent stitch.

14 Centre: Work five long stitches over the top of the centre three rows, then catch together firmly in the centre.

Making Up
1 Cut a piece of velvet the same size as the embroidery, plus a small turning allowance.

2 Tack them together (right sides together).

3 Oversew three of the edges closely.

4 Remove tacking stitches.

5 Turn to right sides.

6 Stuff with kapok.

7 Close up the open edge.

(Sister Alix Binyon - I made this pin cushion whilst recovering from a fall downstairs).

P·A·T·C·H·W·O·R·K

Starfish

Materials
Firm cotton material with distinctive stripe pattern
Sheeps wool for stuffing
A few pearl-headed pins

Method
1 Cut 12 papers using 1″ irregular Pentagon, and two papers using 1″ Hexagon.

2 Using the paper patterns, cut the fabric, making best use of the stripes, allowing a turning.

3 Tack papers to the fabric pieces, turning over the edges.

4 Sew patches together to make the Starfish shape, leaving a gap to turn the pincushion.

5 Remove papers and turn to the other side.

6 Stuff firmly with sheep's wool.

7 Sew up the gap.

8 Decorate the centre with a few pearl headed pins.

(D. Softley)

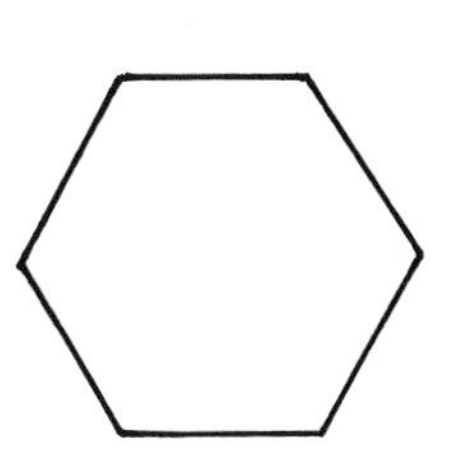

1″ Hexagon

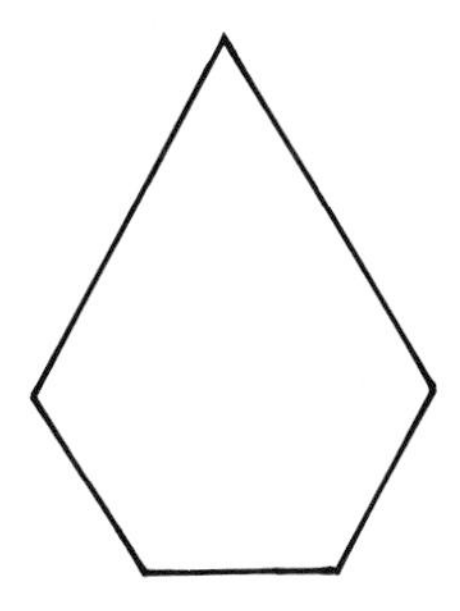

Irregular Pentagon

Patchwork Ball

Materials

Small pieces of plain cotton material in several colours
Oddments of stranded embroidery cotton
Iron-on Vilene
Greaseproof paper for tracing
Dressmakers carbon
Terylene filling

Method

1 Trace a template and use this to cut out 12 patches of cotton material.

2 Trace motifs and transfer one to the centre of each patch with the aid of dressmakers carbon.

3 Embroider each motif with one strand of embroidery cotton, then outline each motif with a line of stem stitch.

4 Trace the centre section of the template and use this as a pattern to cut out 12 iron-on Vilene patches.

5 Iron one to the centre back of each embroidered patch.

6 Tack turnings neatly to the underside of the patches.

7 Sew six patches together with oversewing stitches, on the wrong side of the work, then sew the side slits together to form a cup. This is half of the ball.

8 Make up the remaining six patches in the same way, then sew the two cups together, fitting the points of the patches carefully leaving one small opening to insert the filling.

9 Fill firmly and sew up the opening with ladder stitch.

(Joyce Routledge)

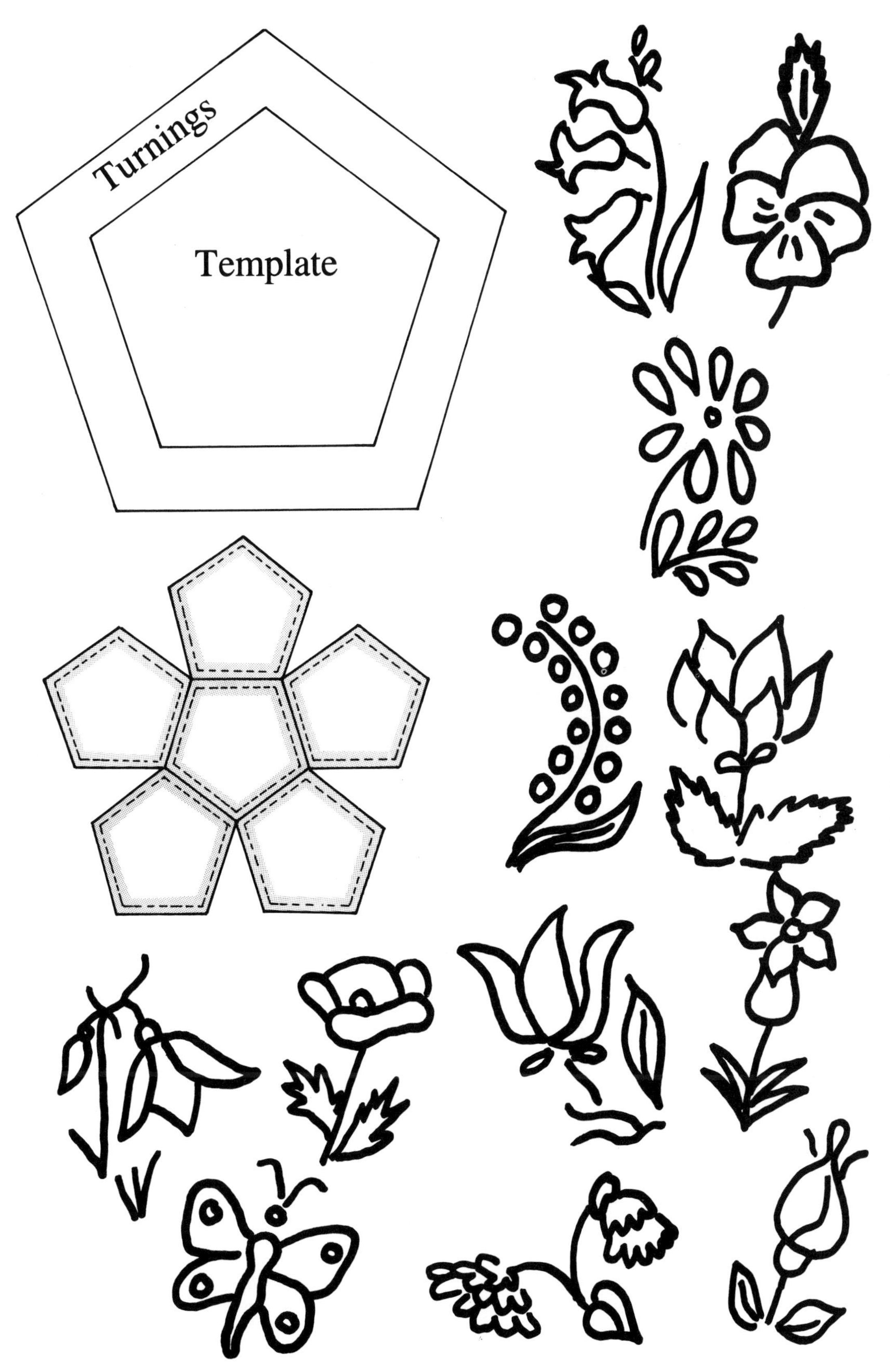
Turnings
Template

The Great Dodecahedron

Method

1 Using the template (stick on to card or plastic) cut out 60 triangles from thin card (eg. post card).

2 Pad these triangles with wincyette. It is easier to cut out the wincyette after sticking the triangles on with a glue stick.

3 Assemble a collection of toning or contrasting coloured materials, in silk or Libertay Lawn. Fine natural materials are easier to work with.

4 Cover all the triangles. Stick the turnings over on to the wrong side using a glue stick.

5 Stitch together in threes on the wrong side using a small over-sewing stitch.

6 Stitch these units together using COTON A BRODER in a contrasting colour, and employing FLY STITCH.

7 Leave the final unit, or two, open and stuff pincushion with toy filling or sheeps wool. Do not over stuff or the shapes will distort.

8 Finally, stick glass headed pins through sequins and push into the points, also stick pins along the edges.

(Madeleine Howard)

Dotted lines: sew on wrong side.
Solid lines: sew on RIGHT side.

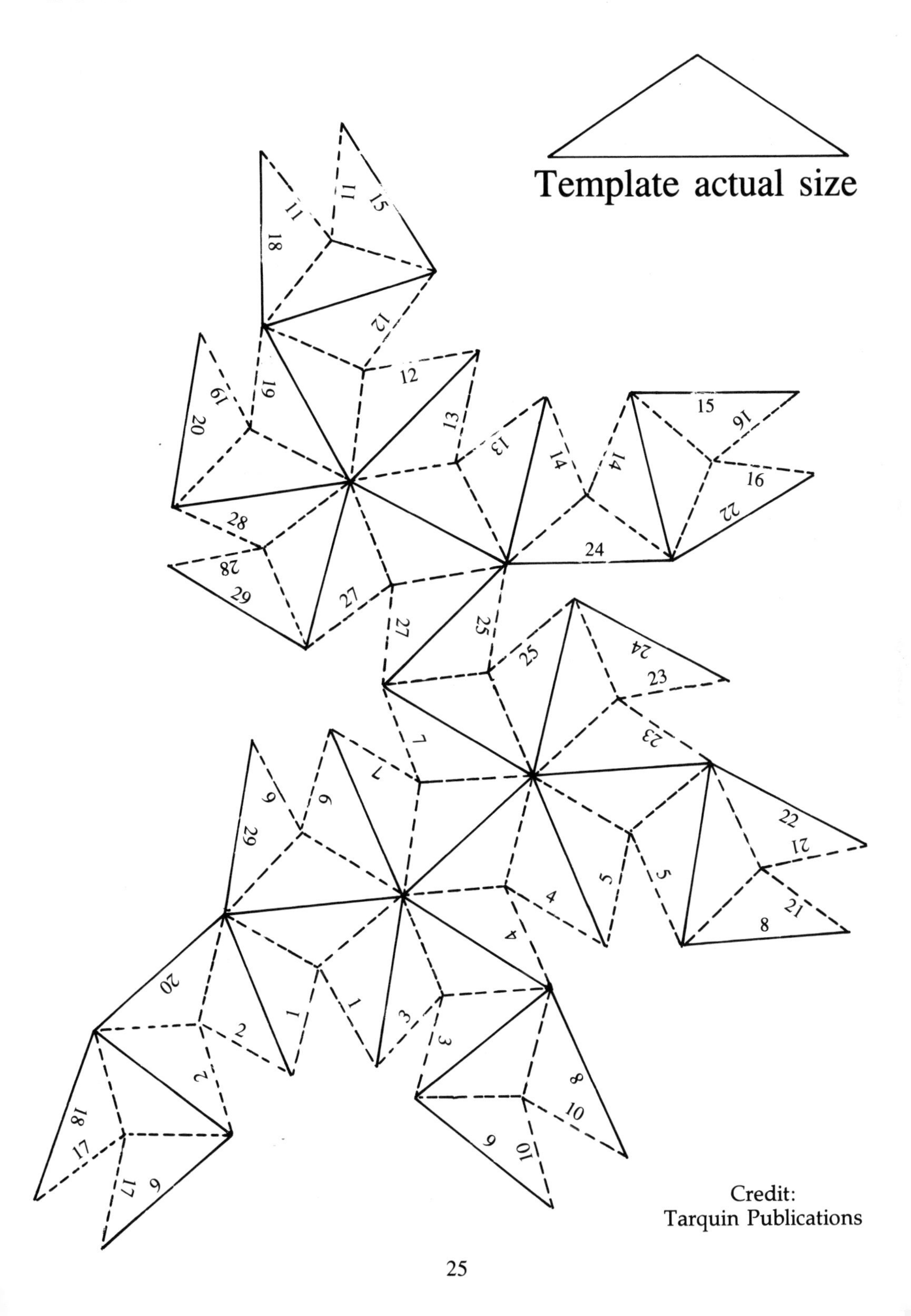

Cathedral Window

Method

1 Cut two squares of fabric about twice the size of the required pin-cushion.

2 Turn in ¼″ all around and tack on each.

3 Fold all corners to the centre, precisely, then repeat and press, stitch down.

4 Repeat on 2nd square.

5 Oversew these two folded squares together on the wrong side.

6 Cut a small square of contrasting fabric, (or this can be emb.) Pin this over centre seam of the 2 squares, then turn folded edges of the square over the small centre patch.

7 Stitch along layers to form a "frame".

8 On wrong side sew together the two short sides, fold again so that the small patterned square lies in the centre of cushion. Join a to b then c to b. Join d to e then f to e. Join b to e **after** stuffing the pincushion firmly.

(Joan Appleton Fisher)

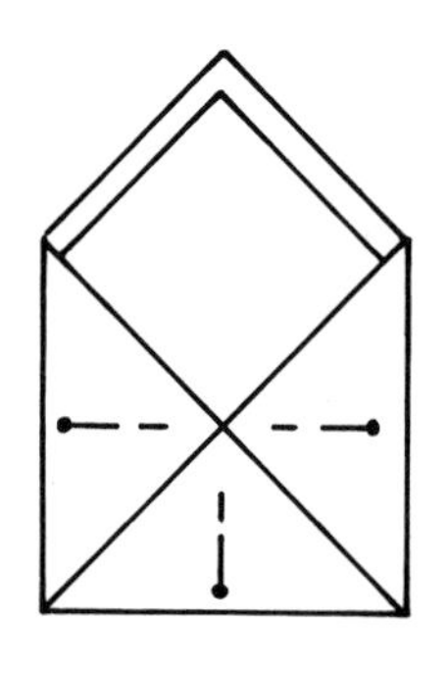

Hexagon Star

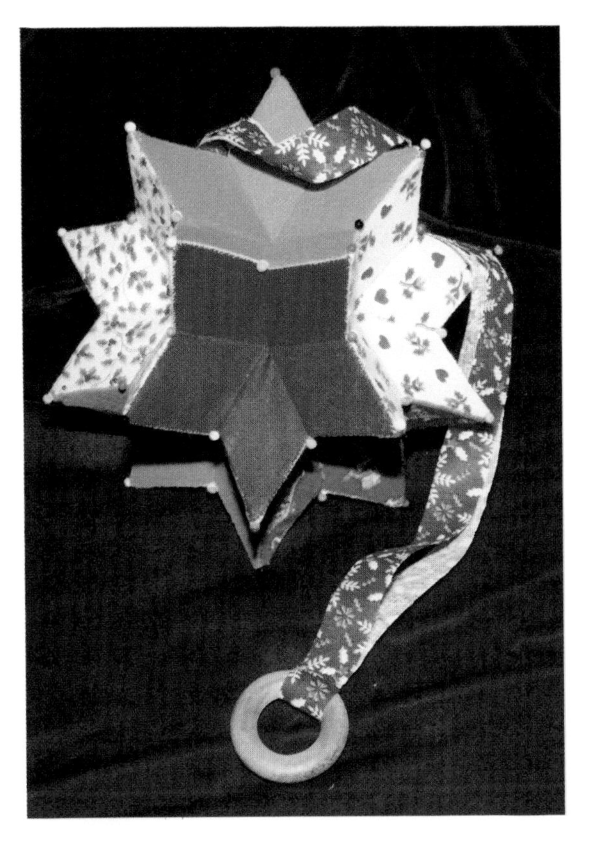

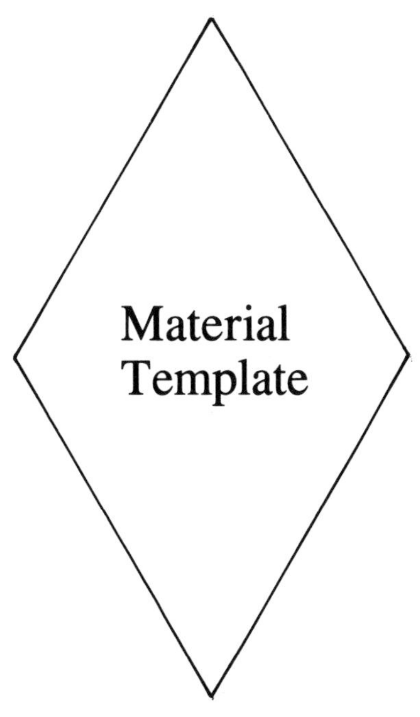

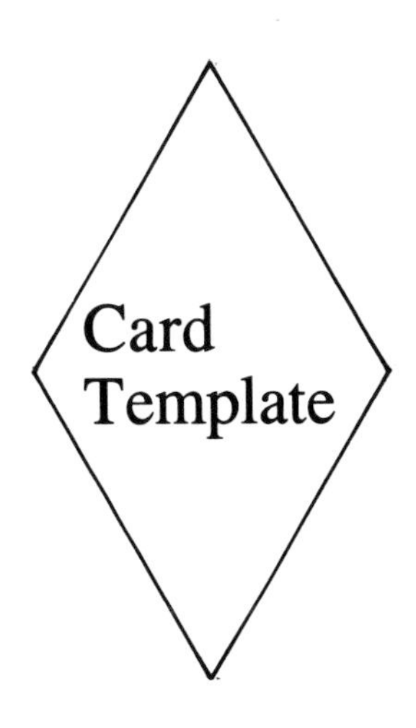

This design dates from the 19th Century. It takes 60 haxagon diamonds with cardboard shapes left in the patches. The diamonds are assembled in groups of five and then the stars are joined in hexagon shapes.

Method

1 Using any small sized diamond template, cut material to cover card.

2 Cover and tack onto the card.

3 Press with warm iron.

4 Sew 5 diamonds together to make a star.

5 Sew the stars together.

6 Remove the tacking stitches **after** filling the star shape with stuffing.

7 Add a ribbon if the pin cushion is to be used as a decorative item.

(Alison Minter)

N·O·S·T·A·L·G·I·C

Satin Heart Secret

Materials
15″ (38cm) square satin
1 yard peach and cream lace
Short lengths of lace, ribbon and braids
Small beads
Small amount of stuffing

Method
1 Cut two hearts and two pockets. Put the two pocket pieces wrong sides together and tack all round.

2 Cut a strip of satin 2″ (5cm) x 8″ (20cm) and bind top edge of pocket.

3 Tack pocket to right side of one piece of heart.

4 Take the remaining heart shape and the peach and cream ribbon and, keeping the two laces together, pleat the lace around the edge of the heart, frill facing inwards.

5 Take the two heart shapes and put them together, with right sides together, tack and then machine around edge leaving a gap down one side.

6 Turn to the right side and stuff firmly, slip stitch opening together.

7 On front of heart, lightly draw two small heart shapes. Take a piece of lace and pleat around first heart shape.

8 Sew small beads around second heart shape.

9 Stitch braid around outside edge of heart.

10 Turn over and on top edge of pocket stitch some lace and a ribbon bow in the centre. (This pocket is useful for keeping a packet of assorted needles and a thimble in).

11 To finish off, fill centre heart with ribbon roses. Also put one on each side of top centre of heart with ribbon bows and loop.

(Yvonne Rowland)

(Diagrams on next page).

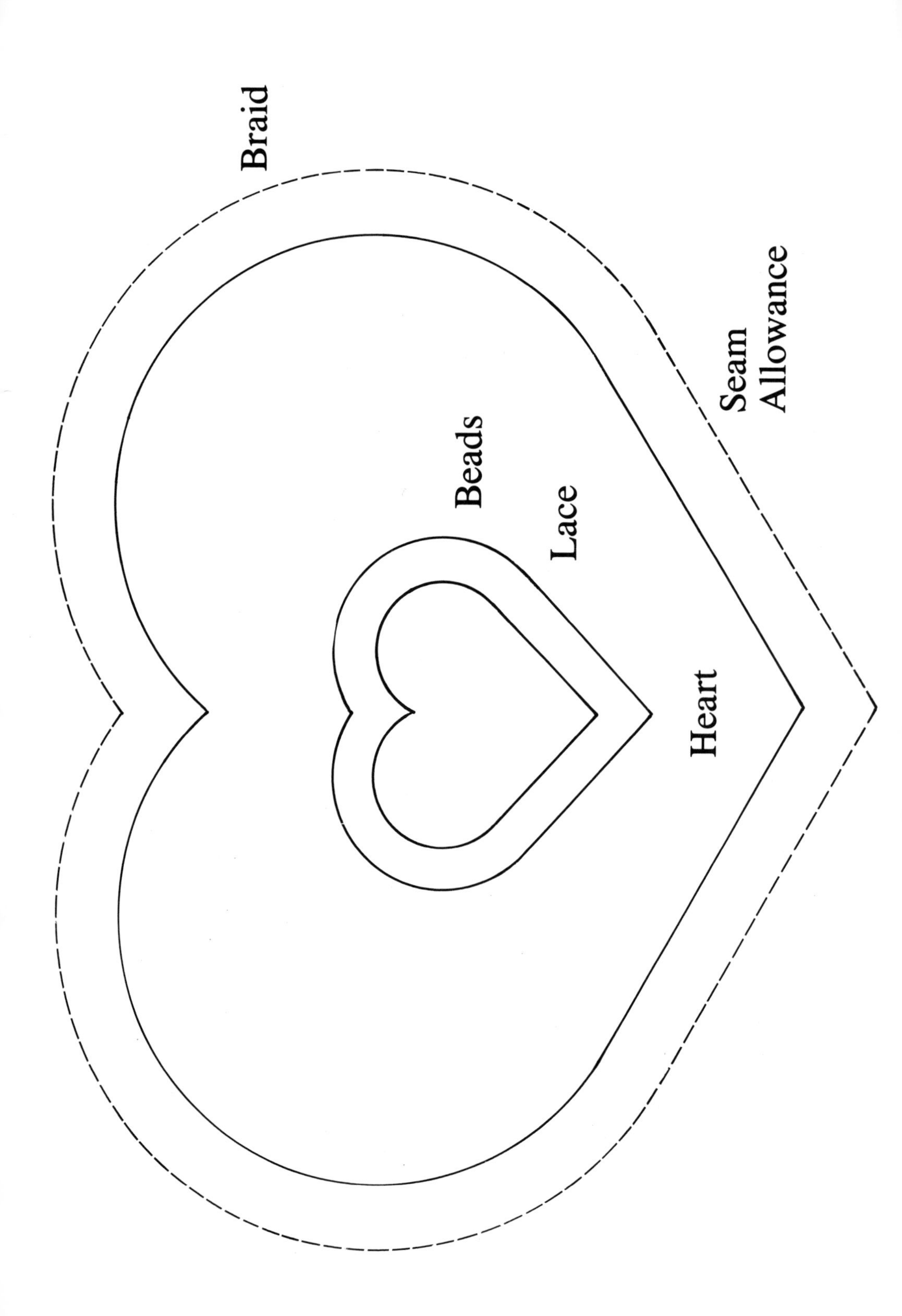
Braid
Seam Allowance
Beads
Lace
Heart

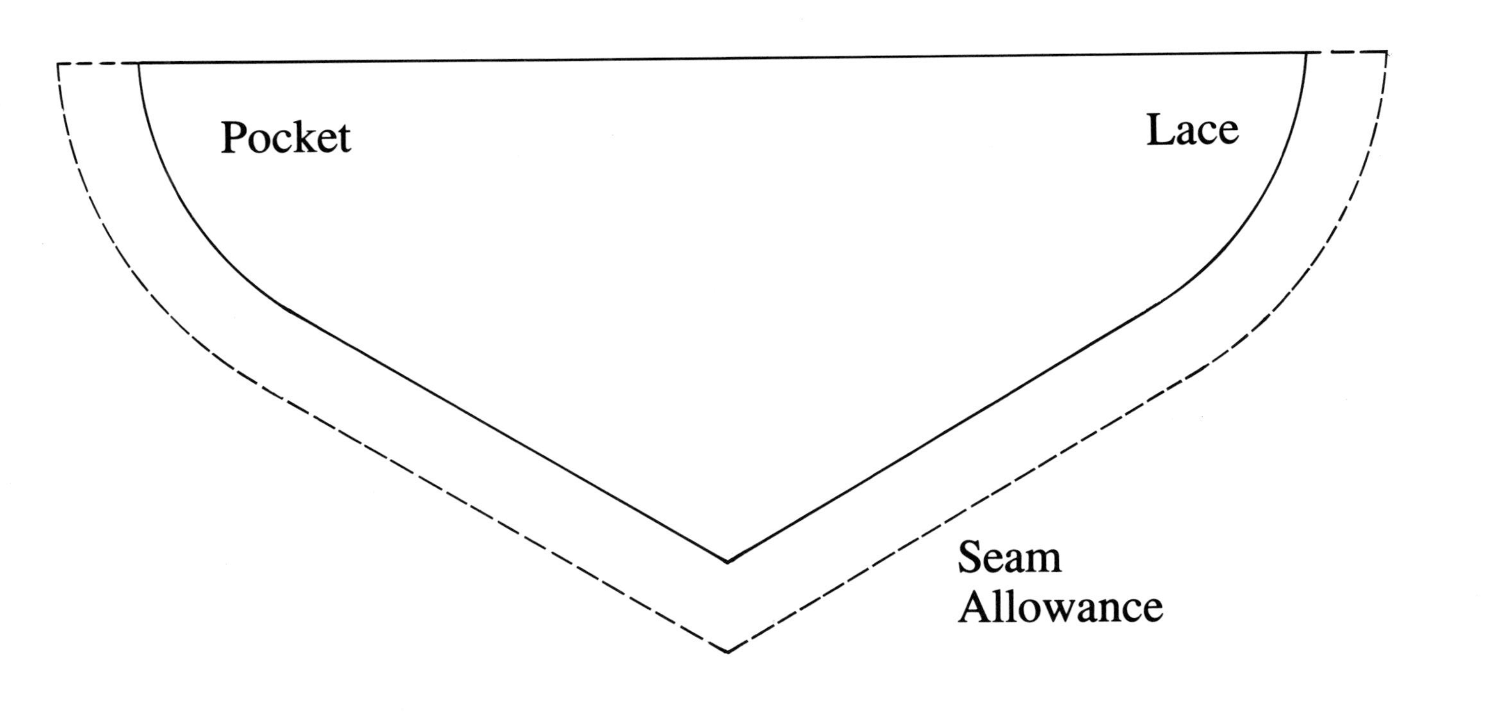

ACTUAL SIZE PATTERN

Victorian Posy

Materials
Satin
Embroidery thread
Lace - bought or hand-made
Sewing thread
Calico
Chopped sheeps wool
Compass
Transfer pencil

Method
1 With the compass, draw a circle with a radius of 55cm. Inside the circle inscribe two more with a radius of 40 cms and 25 cms. (A larger pincushion can be made with more bands for flowers).

2 With a new piece of tracing paper, mark in vague outlines of flowers in the bands, using a transfer pencil.

3 Iron the design onto the satin and embroider the flowers and leaves.

To make the inner cover:
4 Make a round pillow out of calico, the same size at the top and bottom as the outer compass circle of the top.

5 Join the top and bottom with a side band and leaving an opening for stuffing.

6 Stuff pincushion and slip stitch opening together.

Outer cover
1 Join the embroidered top to a side band a little deeper than the calico one, with hand sewing.

2 Gather the long bottom edge of side band.

3 Place the top satin cover over the calico cushion and gather the satin side band over the bottom edge.

4 Stitch the satin underpiece, lacing in the edges.

5 Slip stitch lace over seams around top.

(M. Poorun)

Beaded Star

Materials
15cm x 30cm White Cotton Fabric
Pearl Beads
Cream Stranded Cotton
50cm White Lace
Sewing Thread and Filling

Method
1 From fabric cut 2 circles 14 cm in diameter.

2 Copy the design onto the right side of one circle.

3 Sew small pearl beads along the lines in split stitch using two strands of cream stranded cotton.

4 With wrong sides together, sew the two circles together leaving a small opening.

5 Turn right side out, fill and sew up opening.

6 Sew a bead to the centre of each side, pulling tightly to draw it in.

7 To finish, sew a length of gathered lace around the edge.

(Wendy Brown)

Victorian Style Pincushion

Materials
Two pieces of velvet approx. 5″ x 6″
Sawdust
1 metre/yd velvet ribbon
Box of 1″ steel dressmaker pins
Assorted beads, sequins
Lace edging

Method
1 Cut two rectangles of velvet and machine right sides together round edge, leaving a gap.

2 Turn through to the right side and stuff VERY firmly with sawdust. Sew up.

3 Sew lace around edge.

4 Cut velvet ribbon in half. Make one half into loops and attach to long top edge in front of lace.

5 Cut other half in two and attach at lower edge to form streamers.

6 Make a motif for the centre from a scrap of lace.

7 Decorate with pins threaded first with a small bead, then larger beads and sequins in different colours and shapes etc.

(G Ramsey)

Victorian Pincushion

Materials
Square of firm, strong material (e.g. Velvet) 6″ (or less)
Sawdust for stuffing
Length of fringing or lace
UHU glue

Method
1 Fold material across corner to corner to form a triangle, right sides together.

2 Sew up both sides leaving a gap in the centre of one side to enable it to be turned.

3 Turn right side out and stuff with sawdust to make as firm as a rock. Use blunt end of a pencil to fill in the corners.

4 Sew up the gap using strong thread, forcing the two corners together on each side of the fold. The crease should 'pleat' across in attractive lines. This will be very difficult.

5 Decorate around the seam using fringing or lace. If it is difficult to sew on trimming, use UHU glue.

6 Decorate with pins, sequins or pearls as desired.

This 'Victorian' pin cushion has raised money for our local lifeboat and one of the ladies involved with their society showed me how to do them. Since then I have made many for the Christchurch Lace Society sales table.

(Ruth Croston)

White Lace Basket

A miniature basket can become a most charming and sturdy Pincushion. My example has been covered in a plain white cotton fabric for an ''Old-Fashioned'' look. Satin bows adorn the handle, and I have trimmed the frills with my own Bobbin Lace, worked in an old Bedfordshire design. The Pincushion is filled with emery powder to polish and sharpen the pins. This basket, however, would look equally attractive if a printed fabric was chosen and silk flowers instead of bows.

N.B. The emery powder also acts as a weight.

Method

1 Measure the **inside** of the basket, including the width of the rim.
Cut out a circle in Calico, using your measurement as its diamater.

2 Measure across the **top** of the basket, including the width of the rim.
Cut out a circle in Calico and a circle in your chosen fabric, using your measurement as its diamater.

3 Measure the circumference of your basket.
Cut out two strips in chosen fabric, using your measurement as the length of each. The width of the strips will depend upon the depth of frill required.

4 Hem each strip along one edge and both ends.
Place two rows of gathering stitches along the other edge.

5 Fold each circle of fabric in half, cut out a notch at each end of the fold, no deeper than half the width of the baskets rim.

6 Place two rows of gathering stitches from notch to notch on each side of the larger circle.

7 Place circle of chosen fabric (right side facing) over Calico circle of same size. Match notches and tack together.

8 Place smaller circles (chosen fabric facing) over larger circle. Match notches and pull gathering stitches up to meet the smaller circles. Sew a firm seam, leaving a gap behind one of the notches.

9 Pull up gathering stitches on each strip and sew in place between notches.

10 Make a small paper funnel and insert it into the gap left at notch. Pour emery powder into the "sack" until it is packed quite firmly. Complete the seam over the gap.

11 Bind rough edges down with the bias binding.

12 Insert the whole thing into the basket, placing the position of the notches behind the handle each side. Thus, allowing the frills to turn outward, over the sides.

13 Trim frills and handle as required.

(Shirley Bartholomew)

Red Rose Basket

Materials
Small basket
Piece of green velvet
Silk roses
Sheeps wool for stuffing
A few pearl head pins

Method
1 Cut a circle of velvet, depending on the size of the basket chosen.

2 Run a line of gathering stitches around the circle and draw in.

3 Stuff the resultant bag with sheeps wool - if available - and draw the stitches tight.

4 Put a thin layer of Glue (Uhu) around the top of the basket and push the cushion in to make a snug fit.

5 Pin Ribbon Roses around the edge of the pin cushion with pearl head pins and put a few pins in centre

(D. Softley)

Rose Basket

Materials

1 Basket, 9 cms diameter across the top
Oddment of cotton fabric for the pad
2m of each of two colours of 1 cm wide ribbon, to tone with fabric
1m each of three colours of narrow (2/3mm) ribbon, to tone with fabric
8 small beads
Small amount of stuffing
Sewing cotton to match fabric and ribbon
Pins

Method

1 Cut a 20 cm diameter circle of fabric.

2 Run a gathering thread approx 1 cm inside the edge and pull up slightly.

3 Stuff the pad, pull up the gathers so that the pad fits securely inside the basket then fasten off.

4 Make the roses from 18 cm lengths of the 1 cm wide ribbon. Fold down raw edge diagonally then roll into a small tube (about 3-4 'turns' of ribbon). Secure with a few stitches.

5 To form the first petal, fold the ribbon down diagonally towards you and roll the tube across it until the width of the tube lies flat against the width of the ribbon again. Secure with a few stitches. Continue this way spacing the petals evenly as you go. To finish turn in the raw edge twice and catch down to neaten.

6 Make 9 roses from each colour to go round the top of the basket and 1 extra for the handle. Stitch the roses to the pad alternating the colours and securing every other one to the basket to hold the pad in place.

7 Cut 2 x 30 cm strips from each strip of narrow ribbon. Take 1 piece of each colour and tie around handle, secure with a few stitches and add beads. Trim ends of ribbon and repeat on other side of basket.

8 To make the handle decoration cut 35 cm length of narrow ribbon, twist into 'figure of eight' loops. Switch to secure and continue until a 'circle' of loops is formed. Stitch to the handle and then stitch rose to the bow.

(Gillian Borrett)

(Further details on how to make roses are on p.105).

A·N·I·M·A·L·S

Sheep in the Meadow

Materials
7″ x 6″ piece of best quality canvas, 14 holes to the inch
Small amount of any white wool
Small amount of black thread
2 small beads for eyes and beading needle
The following threads in D.M.C. coton perle size 5: sky blue, white, corn colour, 6 shades of green from light, medium to dark

Method
1 Sky - tent stitch over one thread.
2 Clouds - back stitches over two threads.
3 Background of hills - tent stitch.
4 Tree - leaf stitch.
5 Corn - uneven straight stitches.
6 Sheep - French knots.
7 Face and legs - black thread.
8 Field in shades of brick stitch.

Making up
1 Leaving corners, work 3 rows of brick stitch over 4 threads, then backstitch over 2 threads on last row.

2 Join corners together.

3 Cut stiff card the same size as top of the work, stick fabric over it.

4 Stuff pin cushion with wool or wadding.

5 Stitch base firmly to base of cushion.

(Cynthia Kendzior)

Hedgehog

Materials
Brown Velvet 20cm x 10cm
Brown Felt 20cm x 5 cm
2 small black beads
Approx 3 heaped tablespoons of clean sand

Method
1 Trace the face pattern and pin to felt.

2 Cut out, using pinking shears, for the shaped edge.

3 Machine felt to velvet along shaped edge.

4 Sew the beads through both fabrics as eyes.

5 Fold the piece in half, right sides together, and machine through all thicknesses to make a cone.

6 With work still inside out, fold cone to form a triangle.

7 Machine across from the mid points of each side.

8 Turn right side out and tuck in raw edges.

9 Flatten one corner and oversew securely.

10 Use a funnel in the other corner to fill the hedgehog with sand. It should still be quite floppy.

11 Oversew this corner as before.

12 Hold the hedgehog nose down and shake all sand into the head.

13 Fold the two oversewn edges to meet on the felt seam. Oversew these two seams together securely.

14 Plump hedgehog into a pleasing shape and add his 'prickles'.

(Susan Rescorla)

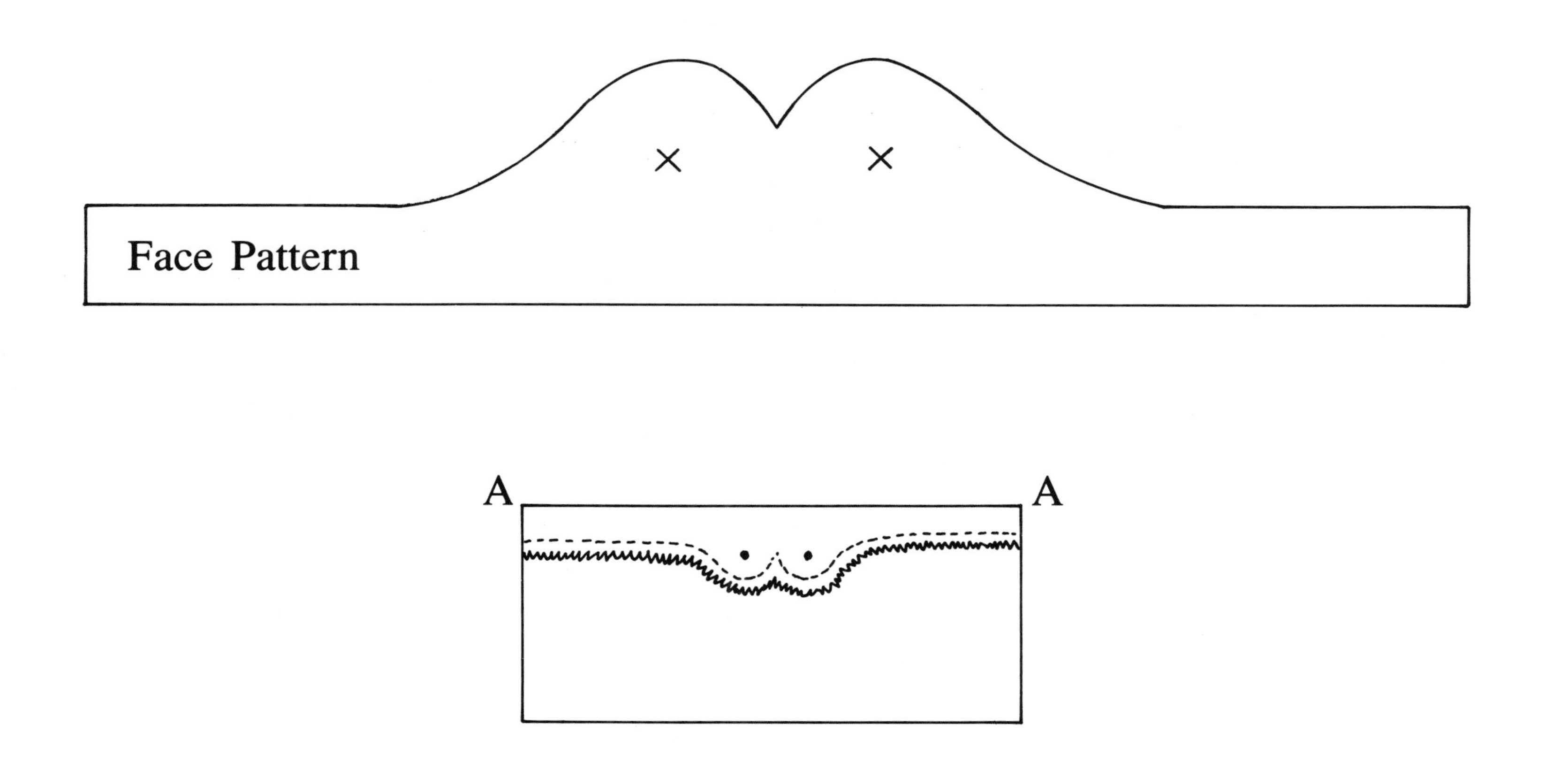
Face Pattern
A
A

Puppy on a Cushion

Materials required:
Small piece of cotton fabric and felt
Length of narrow lace, approx 18 ins long (45 cms)
Small ribbon bow
Stuffing
Copydex

Pincushion
1 Cut two pincushion pieces from cotton fabric, allowing ¼″ seams.

2 With right sides together, stitch edges leaving an opening for turning.

3 Clip curves in seam, turn right side out.

4 Stuff firmly and close opening. Sew lace around edges.

Puppy
1 Cut pieces from felt. Join seams from A to B on main body, leaving an opening for turning, as indicated.

2 Fold face over, matching C to AA and sew face to body.

3 Flatten and sew rear.

4 Turn right side out, stuff and close opening.

5 Embroider features on face.

6 Glue: ears to side of head; main body to base; base to pincushion.

7 Sew bow to top of head.

(Brenda Daniell)

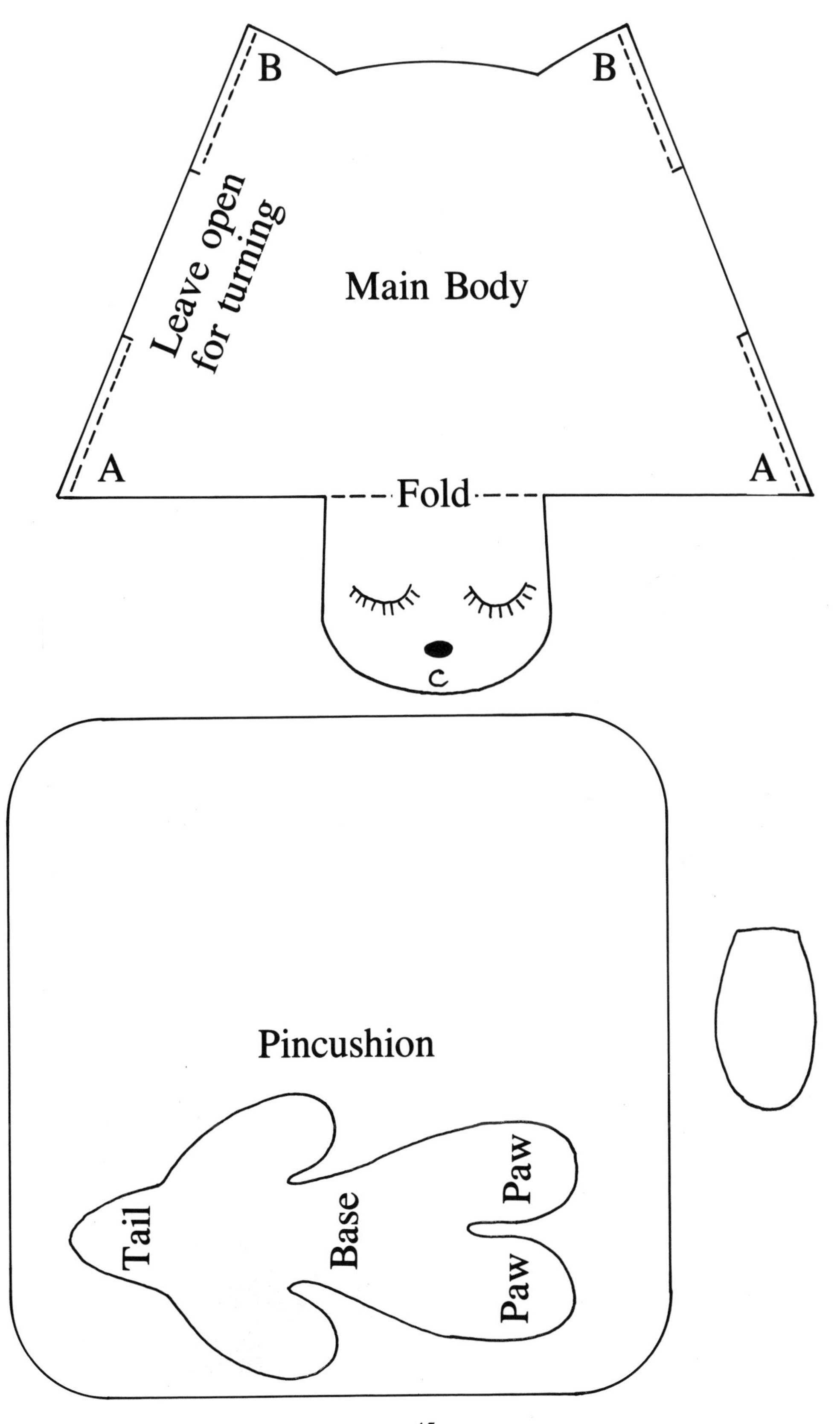
B
B
Leave open
for turning
Main Body
A
A
Fold
Pincushion
Tail
Base
Paw
Paw

Tortoises

Materials
Felt: 1st colour - 20 cms x 30 cms
2nd colour - 20 cms x 30 cms
3rd colour - 8 cms x 10 cms
4th colour - 6 cms x 6 cms
Plus scraps of White, Blue, Red and Black
Kapok or polyester stuffing
Pearl headed pins
Fabric adhesives
Top hat (from Craft shop)

Method
1 Trace off pattern pieces and use them to cut the felt pieces:
SHELL - cut 2 (1st colour); SHELL EDGING - cut 2 (1st colour); SIDE HEAD - cut 2 (2nd colour); HEAD GUSSET - cut 1 (2nd colour); UNDERBODY - cut 1 (2nd colour); FOOT - cut 8 (2nd colour); TAIL - cut 2 (2nd colour); EYELID - cut 2 (1st colour); EYES - cut 2 (white); INNER EYE - cut 2 (blue); MOUTH - cut 1 (red); NOSE - cut 1 (black); FLOWER TRIM - cut 6 (3rd colour) and 4 from 4th colour; HEAD DRESS STRIP - cut 2 (3rd colour).
NB. All pieces are stitched RIGHT SIDES together, close to the edges.

2 Stitch the feet together in pairs, leaving straight edges E - F open. Turn and stuff lightly.

3 Stitch the two tail pieces together, leaving straight edges G - F open. Turn and stuff lightly.

4 Using broken lines on the pattern as a guide, pin feet to the underbody matching E's and F's.

5 Pin tail in position between back legs, matching G's and H's.

6 Stitch the upper edges of shell from A - B. Turn, and stitch the lower edge of the shell to the underbody, matching A's and B's, leaving opening at side (see pattern).

7 Turn and stuff firmly, taking care not to stretch the opening. Slip to close.

8 Stitch the two side head pieces to the head gusset from C's to D's. Stitch front of the head from B to C. Turn and stuff firmly.

9 Pin neck edge of the head to the front of the shell, then slip stitch into place. Push a little more filling in, if necessary, to keep the head firm.

10 Stitch the two shell edges pieces together, matching I's and J's.

11 Apply adhesive along the upper edge of the shell edging from I to K and place in position, as indicated on the pattern (broken line).

12 Stick two inner eyes to the two eye whites and attach to each side of the head.

13 Stick eyelids into place.

14 Stick on nose and mouth.

15 Stick straight edges of the two head dress strips onto the top of the head, then two flower trims on top of them.

16 Push a pearl headed pin through the centre of them. (Alternatively, glue a hat on, instead of flower trims).

17 Stick the flower shapes onto the shell, then push a pearl-headed pin into the centre of each.

(Jean Stewart)

(Diagrams are on the next page).

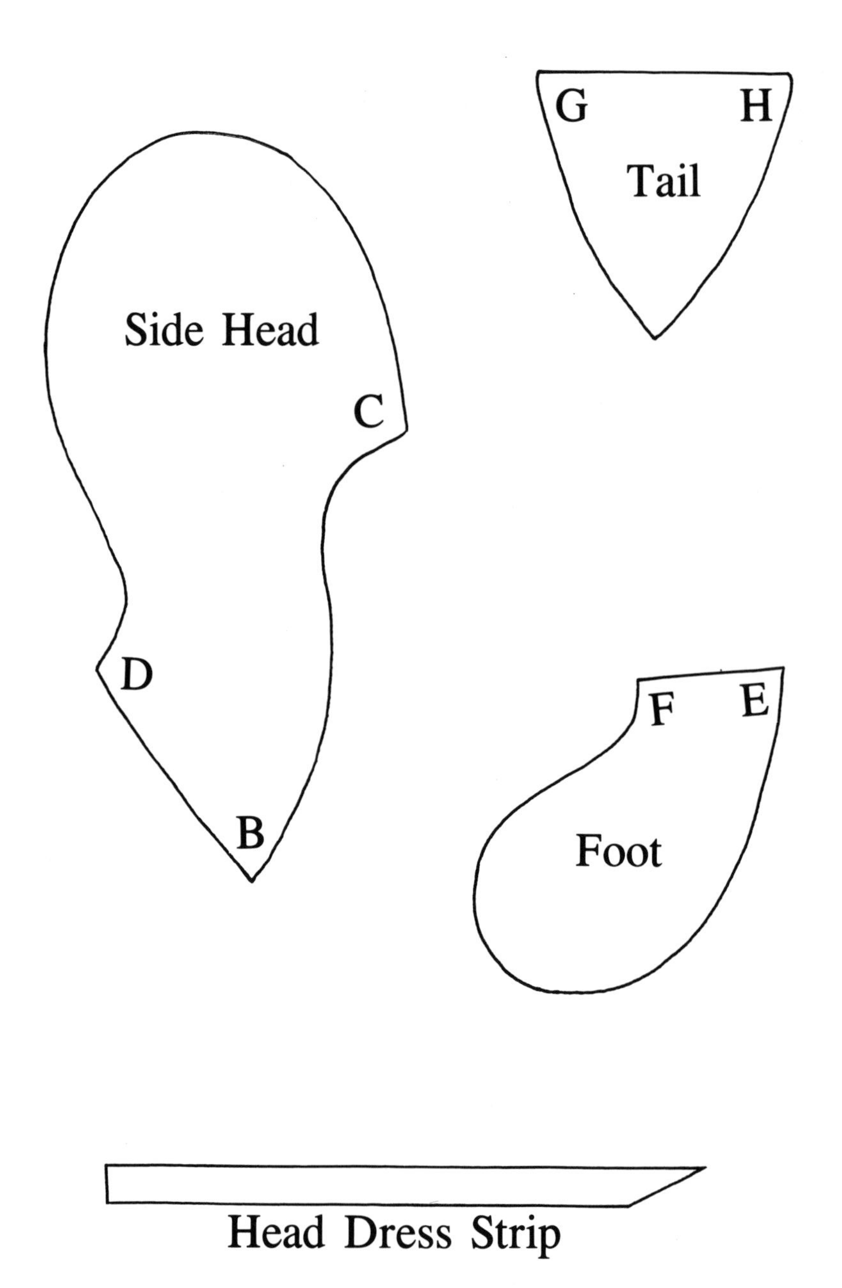
G
H
Tail
Side Head
C
D
B
F
E
Foot
Head Dress Strip

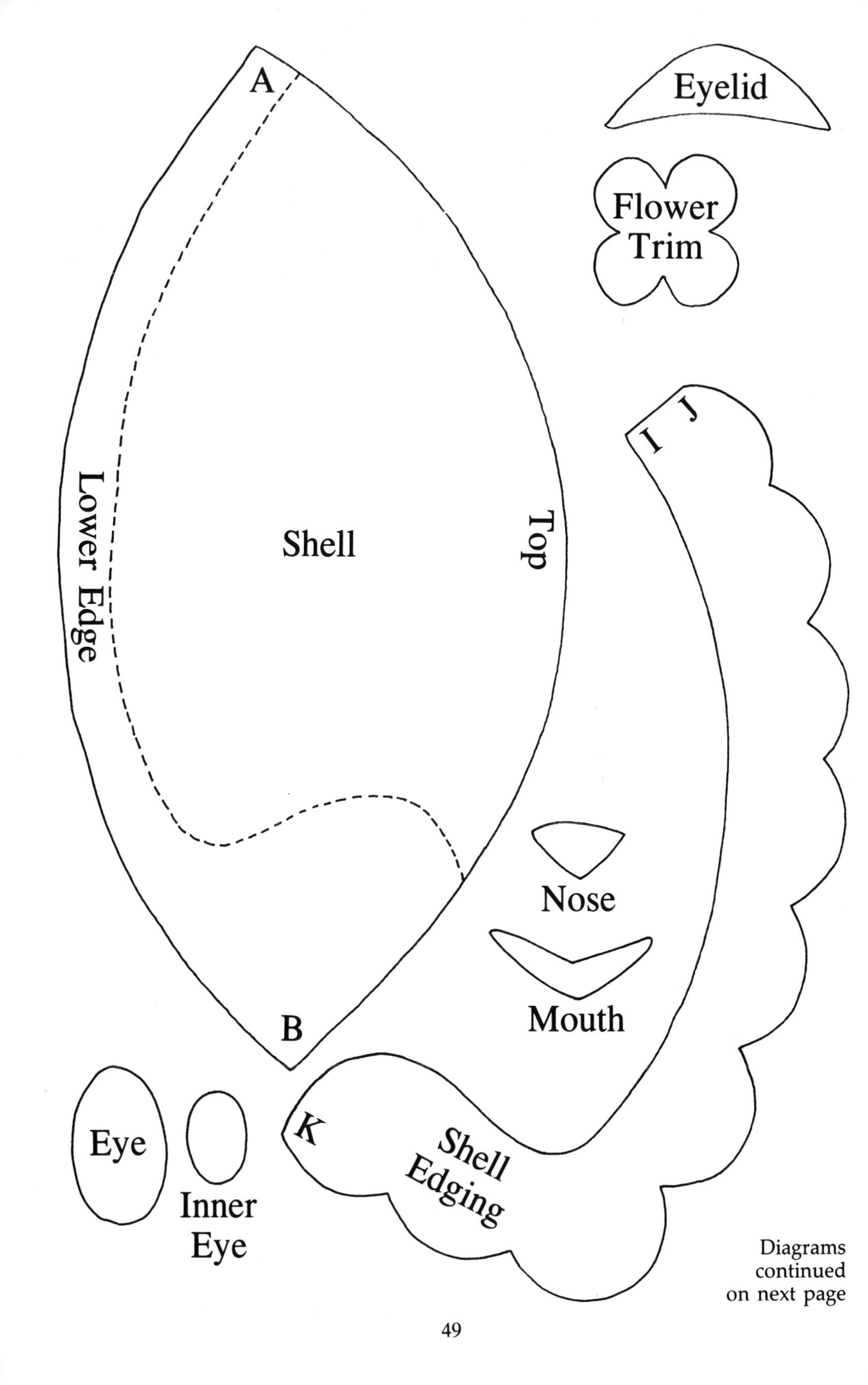

Diagrams continued on next page

Tortoise pattern continued

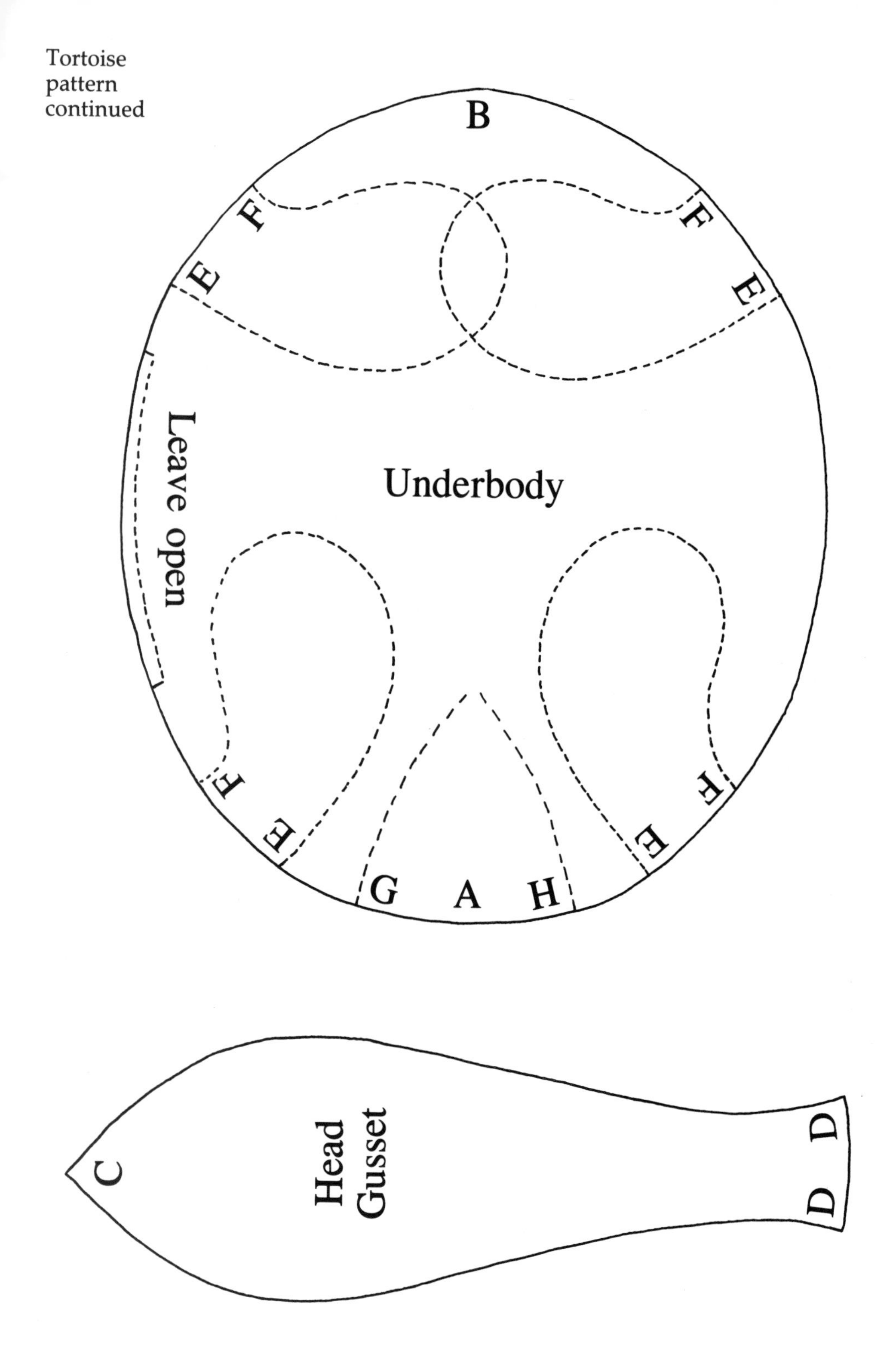

Mouse and Cheese

This pincushion requires patience and neatness. The mouse can be sewn onto the pincushion, or left free standing, to be moved around. Be careful when stuffing the mouse, using only small amounts at a time, pushing gently with a toothpick (or similar). Add more mice if you wish! I have given full instructions for making all the holes, but simpler versions could be made, instead.

Materials

6 cm deep yellow bath sponge, or foam
9 inch square yellow felt
6 inch square red felt
12 inch square white felt
2 x 6 inch long pipecleaners (any colour)
Thin card (for template)
Lightweight iron-on interfacing
15 cm circle of wadding (½ inch thick)
46 cm green narrow ribbon
Yellow, red, white and black cotton
18 cm of 5½ cm wide white velour ribbon (or white felt)
12 cm long piece of pink cord
2 small black beads (for eyes)
Pink felt
Small amount of stuffing
Copydex Glue

Instruction to make the Plate

1 Draw out the patterns for the 14 cm and 15 cm circles.

2 Using the 14 cm pattern cut out one circle in white felt, and another using the ½ inch wadding.

3 Measure 1.5 cm in from the circle edge, marking all round to form another inner circle. This should leave you with a 10.5 cm circle in the centre. Cut all around this circle, but only cutting through half of the thickness of the wadding. Snip

carefully with a pair of sharp scissors across, keeping if possible the same thickness all the way. Try not to pull as you snip, the wadding will otherwise become thin and out of shape. Keep this section.

4 You should now have a dip in the 14 cm wadding circle. The dip should be on the top of the circle. Glue the small cut out section to the underside of the larger circle, making sure that it's central. This forms the base of the plate.

5 Place and pin the felt circle on top. Measure 3.5 cm in from the outside edge, and back stitch all around using white thread. Cut out a 10.5 cm circle in card. Glue this to the underside of the wadding. A 15 cm circle in white felt is then placed underneath. Stab stitch about 2 mm all around.

6 Glue narrow ribbon into place, round edge of plate.

Instructions to make the Cheese

1 Pin and cut out the top, base and main cheese pattern in yellow felt, carefully cutting out the holes. Cut these pattern pieces out again, but this time in a light weight interfacing, making them only slightly smaller in size, than the felt pieces. Place interfacing onto the felt and tack together. Trim back around the holes, so that no excess interfacing can be seen from the outside.

2 Cut out the rind in red felt and another one in the interfacing, allowing extra interfacing at the top. Snip the interfacing at intervals down to the felt to allow for the curve of the cheese. Iron each piece carefully. making sure that the interfacing has adherred itself to the felt.

3 Attach the left side of the rind over the sewing line on the left side of the cheese (red felt on top of the yellow). The interfacing should then be on the wrong side. Sew with small neat back stitches from A - B on the outside using red thread.

4 Stab stitch the base from A - C along to D, in yellow thread along the sewing line. Cast off. Attach the top again using stab stitch, sew from B - F up to G. Do not sew from G - H, but continue sewing from H to E. Cast off.

5 Draw and cut out the base pattern, in thin card. This is used as a template. Draw around it on the piece of sponge/foam with a felt pen. Using a craft knife or sharp scissors, cut out the shape. It doesn't matter if it is a bit uneven, this can be corrected later, with stuffing.

6 Place the cheese pattern pieces around the spong and mark off all the hole positions onto the spong. Repeat for the top as well.

Holes

1 For holes (3) and (6) just cut a slight U-shape into the sponge.

2 For hole (1) which goes right through the cheese, cut around the marked positions only cutting part of the way through, continue to snip right through. Pull excess sponge out, trim off any uneven edges.

3 Hole (2) comes from a small opening at the top and re-appears on the left side of the cheese, with a larger opening. Beginning at the top cut down at the marked position at a slight angle, towards the left. From the side cutting around the marked point to about 1 cm in. The next cut should be of a more upwards cut, in order to meet the top part of the hole. To remove the section of cut sponge pull firmly and discard. You should be able to place a finger from the top down and out of the side. Trim any uneven edges.

4 Holes (4) and (5), simply cut around marked point to about 7 mm in to form the hole. To remove the cut area pull out the sponge, which should then leave you with a clean cup shaped section.

5 Place the sponge into the felt casing. Stab stitch from points D - E in red thread sewing on the stitch line.

6 The top yellow section of the cheese should be placed over the excess interfacing from the red felt (skin). Back stitch in yellow thread about 2 mm from edge, sewing only on the yellow felt, catching the interfacing underneath as you sew from E - B. Change to red thread using back stitch. Sew from B - E, this time only sewing on the red felt (skin). Be careful not to sew the spong as well, cast off.

7 Oversew the last open section A - D in red thread.

8 If the sponge was cut unevenly, and the felt now looks a little lumpy, use small quantities of stuffing, which can be inserted through the felt holes.

9 Using yellow felt cut out shapes for holes (3), (4) and (6) using pattern pieces. Push each into correct positions. To secure over-sew around the edges.

10 For hole (1) place a length of thread around outside edge of the hole. Mark and cut. Using this length as a measurement cut out a rectangle in yellow felt, just enough to go right through the length of the cheese. With a pin apply glue to the top edge of the felt, push together and allow to dry.

This can then be inserted into place, trim off any excess felt. Oversew to secure into place.

Again for hole (5), use a length of thread as a measurement to find the correct length of the rectangle. Cut out and glue edge then insert into the hole, oversew into place.

As hole (2) is more awkward than all the others, the same procedure is used as for hole (5), with the exception of a gap between both felt pieces. You need to cut one rectangle for the top, and a larger rectangle for the side, making them about 1 cm wide. The yellow sponge compensates for this section with no felt covering. Your finger should still be able to enter from the top and out through the side freely.

Instruction to make the Mouse

1 Using pieces of pink felt, cut out the ears, nose, feet and hands, along with 2 white felt arms. Glue one hand onto each arm, in the marked positions.

2 When cutting out the body gusset and the main body pieces, it is useful to place the bottom edge of the pattern onto the velour seam edge. This adds extra strength, needed when turning the mouse inside out, it also prevents the fabric from fraying.

3 Pin the body gusset to one side of the main body. Sew together using running stitch on the wrong side of the fabric about 2 - 3 mm from the edge, sewing from points A to C. Repeat this for the other side. Add head gusset sewing on both sides from points A - E, continuing down to point D.

4 With a pencil carefully push the mouse inside out. Stuff using only small amounts of stuffing at a time. Attach tail, sewing securely into place.

5 For the haunches, using a pin, apply glue to the edges from points C up and around down to D. Place a small amount of stuffing and position onto the mouse, secure temporarily with pins.

6 Cut out a base shape again, using a pin spread some glue around the edge, and fix firmly into place on the underside of the mouse's body.

7 For the eyes, sew on the two small black beads with black thread. To cast off, bring the thread out through the nose enabling you to sew a mouth.

8 Fold the ears in half to form a crease and glue into place.

Instructions to make up Ladder
Note - The ladder is stitched entirely in stab-stitch.

1 Pin and carefully cut out the 2 ladder sections in red felt, and place these together. Stab stitch from A - B continuing on to C.

2 Cut a 9.8 cm length of pipecleaner and insert this into the section just sewn (B - C). Using a piece of left over pipecleaner, cut a 2.5 cm length and fit this into the top rung of the ladder. Stab stitch the square in between the first and the second rung. Repeat this twice to form the rest of the rungs, remembering to insert the lengths of pipecleaner each time.

3 Insert a 9.8 cm length of pipecleaner into the section A - D, which is then sewin in, sew on down to point D, insert the last rung of the ladder - continue to sew from D - C.

To finish off
Place the cheese block across the centre of the plate. Sew firmly into place. Apply a small amount of glue to the bottom of each leg of the ladder, and press firmly into place. Lay ladder towards the cheese attaching it to the cheese with a few stitches. The mouse can either be attached or left loose.

(Linda Hole)

(Postcript from Audrey Babington: There is a little story about this particular pincushion, which my family insist I own up to! I had put ALL the pincushions carefully away, each in a separate plastic bag, in a large suitcase, but failed to notice that I had not fastened it properly. I was not able to continue with the preparation of the book, for several months, as I made a sudden decision to publish "Workbox" magazine quarterly, which involved several major changes in organisation, etc.

When, at last, I was able to turn my attention to the pincushions, I was horrified to discover that a mouse had been in the case, and chewed a hole in practically every plastic bag. To my great relief, all the pincushions were untouched, except one - the mouse and the cheese!

Fortunately, the damage was only minor, and easily rectified. It is intriguing to speculate - was the mouse trying to make friends or was he hoping to eat the cheese?)

Holes (1) Right through the Cheese from left to right side
(2) From the top down to the left side of the cheese
(3) A small indent at the front
(4) only enters about 1cm into the cheese
(5) about 1 cm deep.
(6) an indent on the top right side of cheese

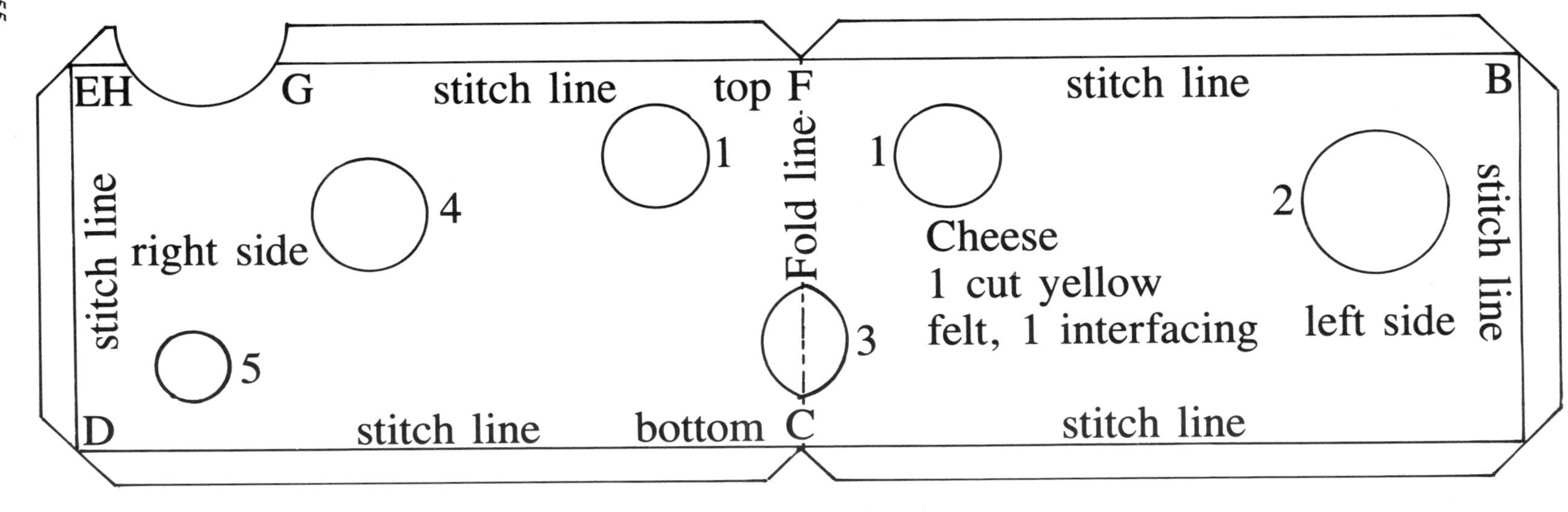

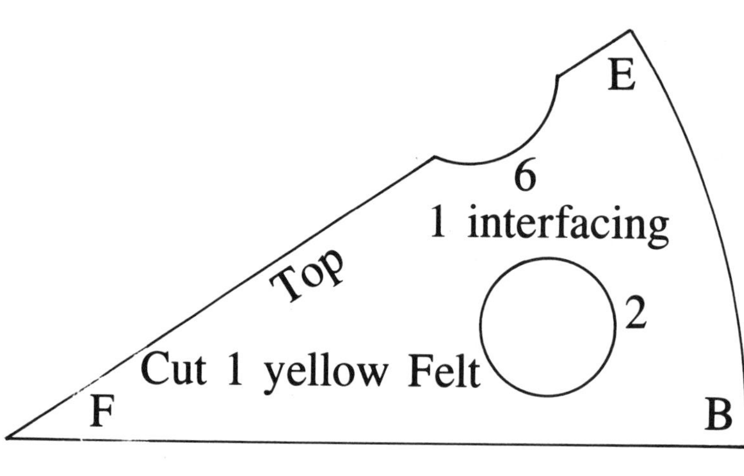

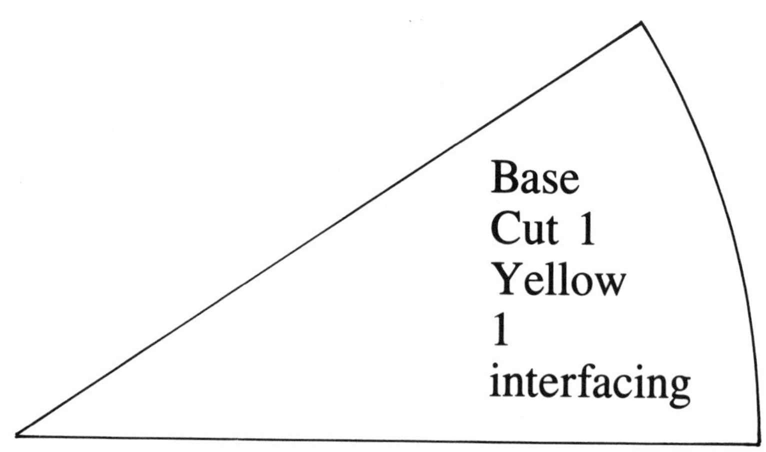

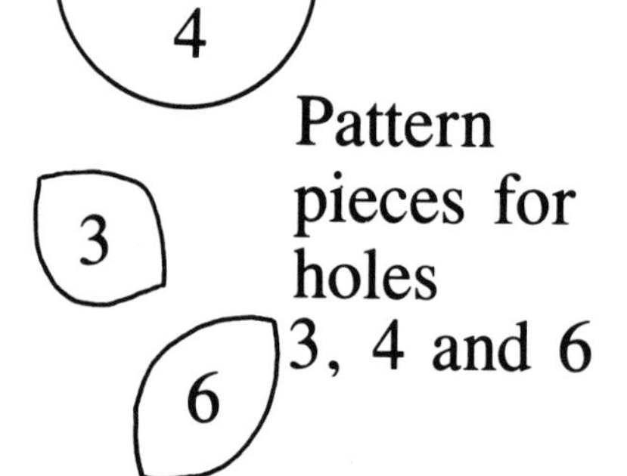

Pattern pieces for holes 3, 4 and 6

B Top E

Left side

Skin
Cut 1 Red Felt
1 interfacing

Right side

A Bottom D

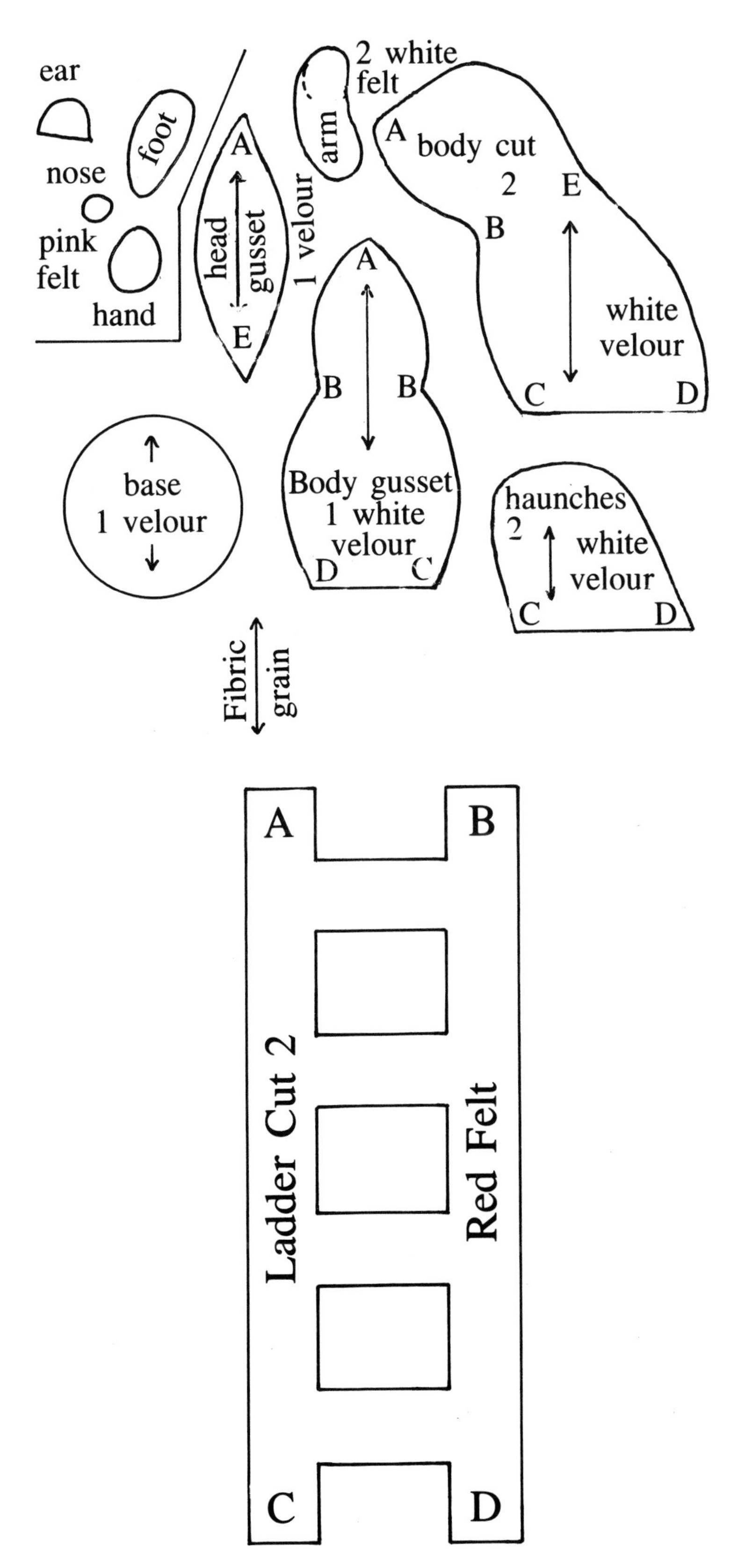
ear
foot
nose
pink
felt
hand
head
gusset
A
E
1 velour
arm
2 white
felt
A
body cut
2
E
B
white
velour
C
D
A
B
B
Body gusset
1 white
velour
D
C
base
1 velour
haunches
2
white
velour
C
D
Fibric
grain
A
B
Ladder Cut 2
Red Felt
C
D

C·H·A·R·A·C·T·E·R·S

Toby Jug

Materials
Small scraps of dress lining and narrow ribbon
Greens, blues and reds for hat and coat
Black, gold, brown, grey or silver for hair
Flesh colour for face
White or cream for collar and froth on beer
Polyester wadding

Method
1 Cut a piece of polyester wadding 5 cm x 80 cm and roll it up tightly into a cylinder shape of 14 cm circumference. Let one end of the cylinder be slightly rounded as this will be the froth on the beer and the pincushion top. Fasten temporarily with a pin.

2 Cut a rectangle of flesh coloured material 16 cm x 7 cm and join the short edges (with right sides facing) taking a 1 cm seam. turn down a 1 cm hem on one raw edge to the wrong side. Make a row of running stitches 3 mm in from other raw edge and leave ends but do not draw up yet. Turn this tube to the right side and pull it over the cylinder of wadding, removing the pin and smoothing it out as you go. Let the 1 cm turning be at the top end and gather up lightly at the bottom to fit round the base.

3 Cut a circle of cardboard 4.4 cm diameter and a circle of material to be used for the coat 6 cm diameter. Run a thread close to the edge of this circle and draw it up round the cardboard circle to cover it and fasten off. Stitch this to the flesh coloured material at the bottom of the jug.

4 Cut a 6 cm diameter circle of cream material and run a gathering thread close to the edge. Place this over the top of the jug and stitch to the turned in top of the flesh material drawing up gathers to fit neatly.

5 Cut a 4 cm x 12 cm rectangle of hair colour material and fold length-ways with right sides facing and stitch ends taking a 1 cm seam sloping slightly towards the fold. Turn right side out and tack raw edges together. Stitch to head with centre back to centre back seam of flesh coloured material with raw edges just under the "froth."

(continued on next page).

6 Cut a 17 cm x 7 cm rectangle of material to be used for hat (preferably on the cross) and join short ends with right sides facing taking a 1 cm seam. Press seam open and fold bringing raw edges together with right side outside and tack edges together. Place hat on head with fold uppermost and raw edges just overlapping stitching round outside of "froth." Stitch 75 mm from raw edge of hat through both thicknesses and through cream froth just above running stitches.

7 Cut a 3 cm x 8 cm rectangle of hat material, preferably crossways, and fold in half longways right sides together. Stitch 75 mm in from folded edge and turn right side out. Place one raw end on centre back seam over hair touching raw edge of hat seam and secure with a few stitches. Turn hat down and fold handle up, stitching through hat to wadding and secure.

8 Cut a 14 cm x 3.5 cm rectangle of cream fabric and fold lengthwise right sides together. Stitch short ends with 1 cm seam and turn right side out and tack raw edges together. Place centre back to centre back of jug and stitch round with raw edges at bottom.

9 Cut a 17 cm x 7 cm rectangle of coat material on the cross and join short edges. Fold as before but tack along centre this time and not at the edge. The seam of this is at the front. Now trim 1 cm off centre front from raw edges tapering to nothing at centre back. Place raw edges to bottom of jug with fold facing downwards and overlap by 1 cm. Stitch through both thicknesses and flesh bottom of jug as near to edge of covered cardboard as possible.

10 Cut a piece of narrow ribbon for necktie about 12 cm and place round neck over coat raw edges and secure in one or two places. Turn up coat and sew a small bow of same ribbon as necktie to centre front catching in coat and strip or ribbon round neck.

11 Neaten remaining edge of handle after trimming to length required and stitch through coat and collar to wadding at centre back.

12 Stitch some eyebrows to match hair, some grey or blue eyes, two tiny dots for nose and a red mouth.

13 Stitch coat bottom to edge of covered circle with small stitches.

Quickie Toby Jug

Method
1 Cut 5 cm from the middle of a toilet roll and fill it with stuffing.

2 Stick a covered cardboard circle to the bottom and cover the top with a circle of cream material glueing it down round the edges.

3 Dress him with short lengths of coloured ribbon. Velvet is good for the hat with a narrow matching piece of brim and for the handle. A wide piece of flesh colour will cover the toilet roll middle keeping the join at centre back which will almost all be covered with the ''clothes''. Use coloured pencils for features.

(Joan Perry)

(see picture p.58)

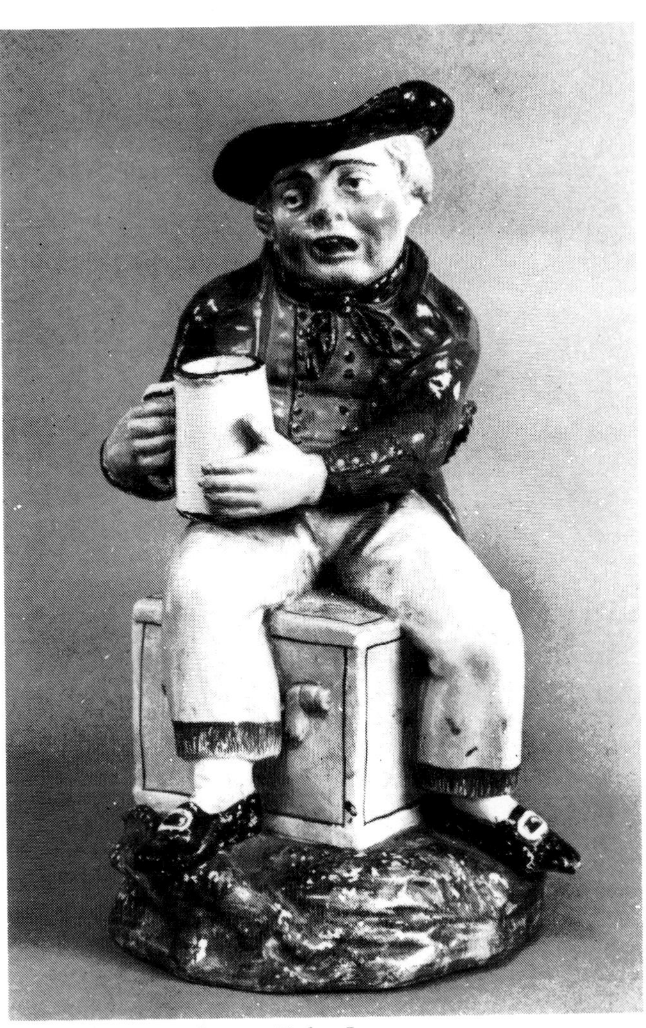

An Enoch Wood type Toby Jug.

Pierrot

Materials
2 pieces of white felt
Gold lurex fabric for hat
Scraps of blue and red felt for features
Black thread
Sheeps wool for stuffing
¼ yard lace for frill

Method
1 Cut 2 ovals of felt for face.

2 Cut 2 pieces of lurex fabric for hat leaving turnings and stitch to face.

3 Mark the features and embroider nose and eye markings. Stitch on eyes and mouth.

4 Stitch the 2 sides together and turn inside out leaving a gap at chin. Stuff firmly and close gap. Add frill.

(S.A. Beal)

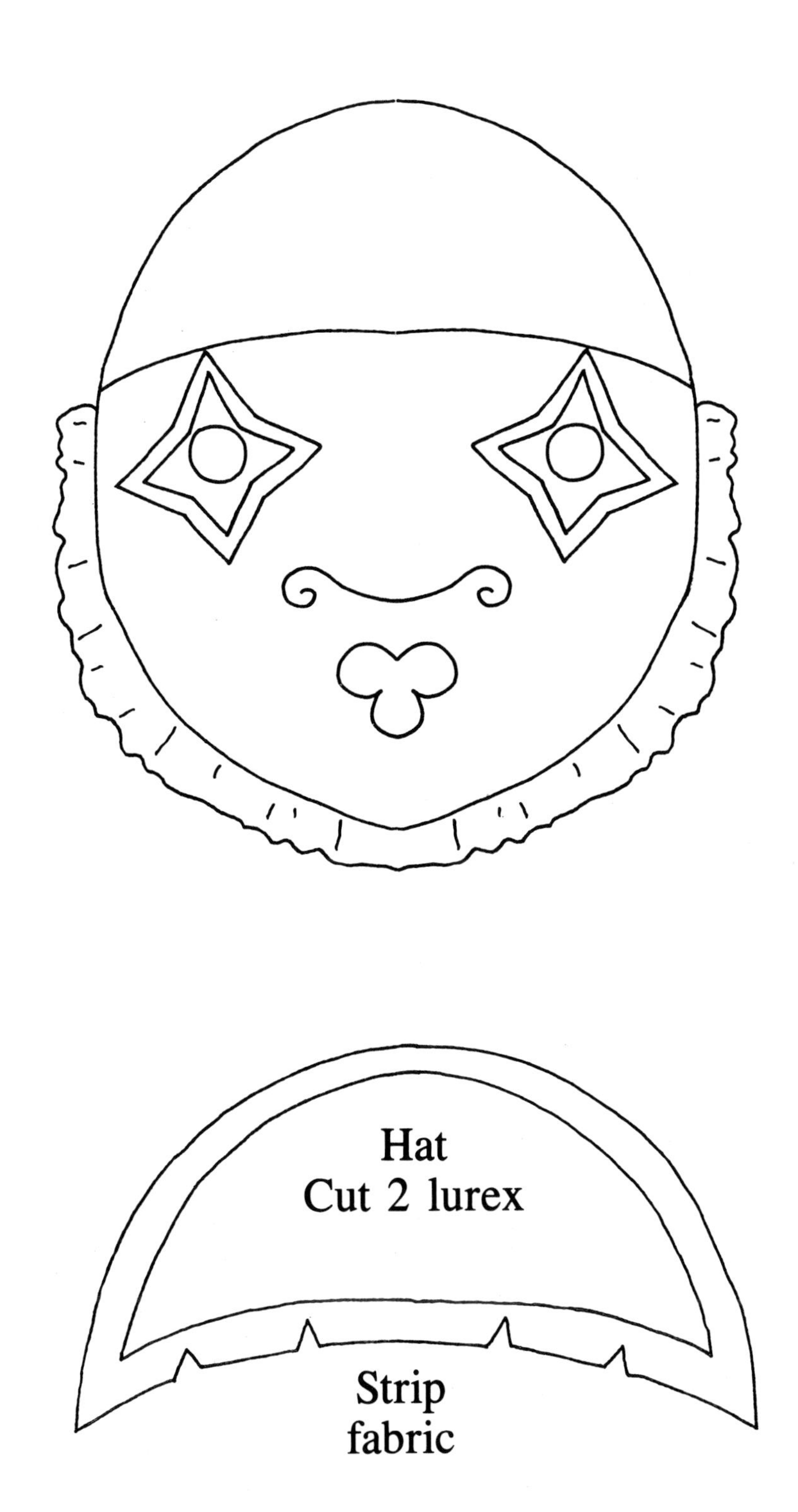
Hat
Cut 2 lurex
Strip
fabric

Punk Pin Cushion

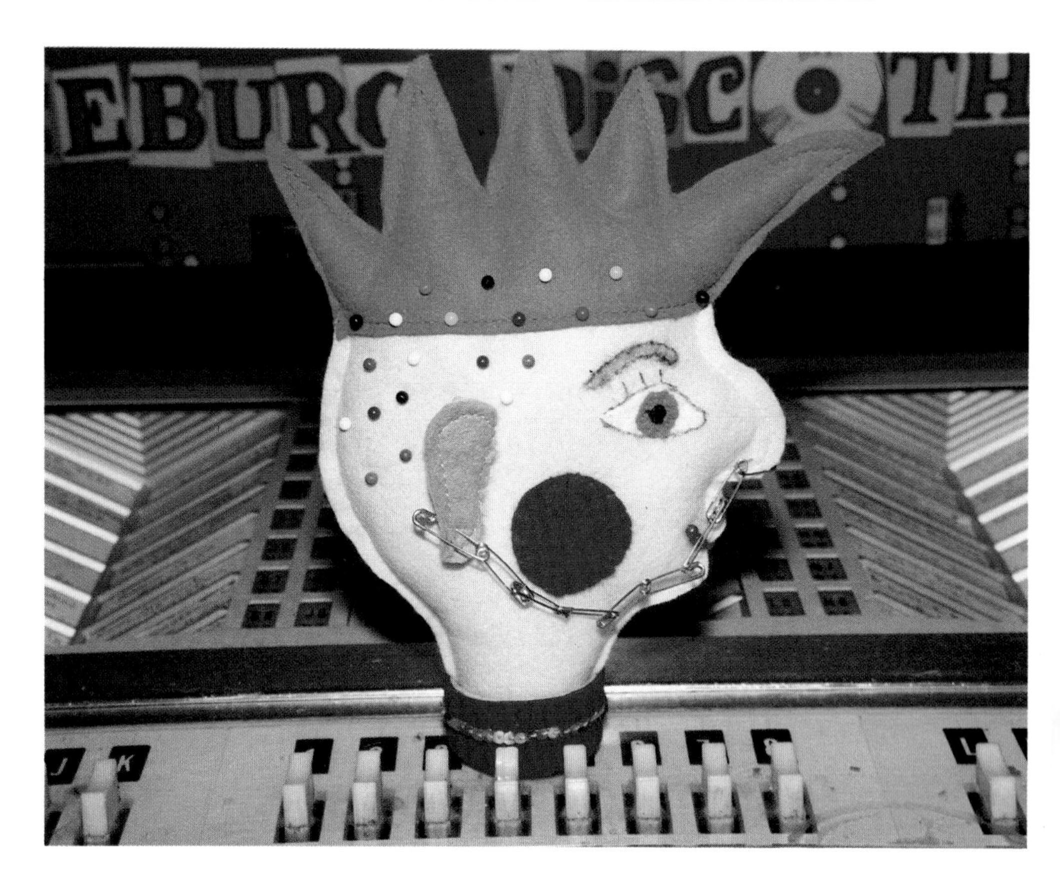

Materials
Sequins or beads
Red & Brown felt tip pens
Fine point black pen
UHU stick or Copydex
Small piece of kitchen roll
Stuffing
1 piece pale pink felt 12″ x 6″ for face
1 piece bright red felt 4″ x 2″ for cheeks
2 pieces any bright colour felt for hair, 7½″ x 4″
1 piece dark pink felt 4″ x 2″ for ears
2 pieces white felt 1¼″ x ¾″)
2 pieces blue felt ¾″ x ¾″) for eyes
2 tiny black circles)
Safety pins and coloured top pins

Method
1 Cut face pattern twice reversing one.

2 Cut hair piece twice.

3 Place on hair piece on top of face piece to dotted line and sew in place, repeat for other side, then sew both together on right side, leaving base of neck open to stuff the head.

4 Glue eyes on to white felt, stitch or glue in place, then stuff the head.

5 Sew over neck opening.

6 Cut 4 ear pieces, sew two together all around, repeat for the other two, position either side of head, slightly curving; stitch in place.

7 Cut two circles 1¼″ diameter out of red felt, glue and sew into place. Use a cotton reel for circles.

8 Cut ⅞″ off empty kitchen roll to act as base. Cover with contact or paint. Squeeze glue inside base, insert neck and leave to dry.

9 Place sequins around collar, link safety pins and attach to ear and nose, stick coloured pins to head back and around hair piece.

10 Mark eyebrows and mouth.

(P. Brown)

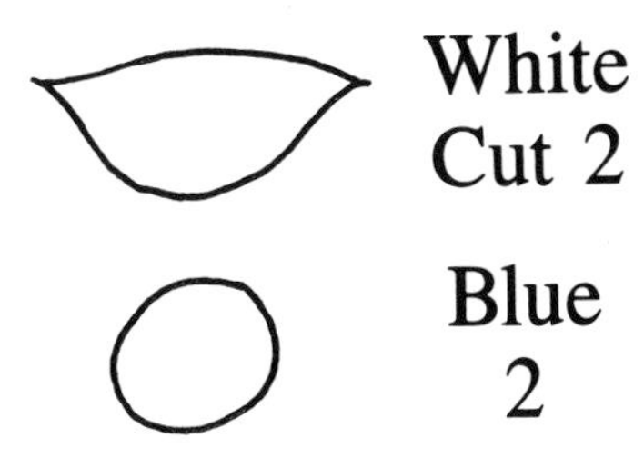

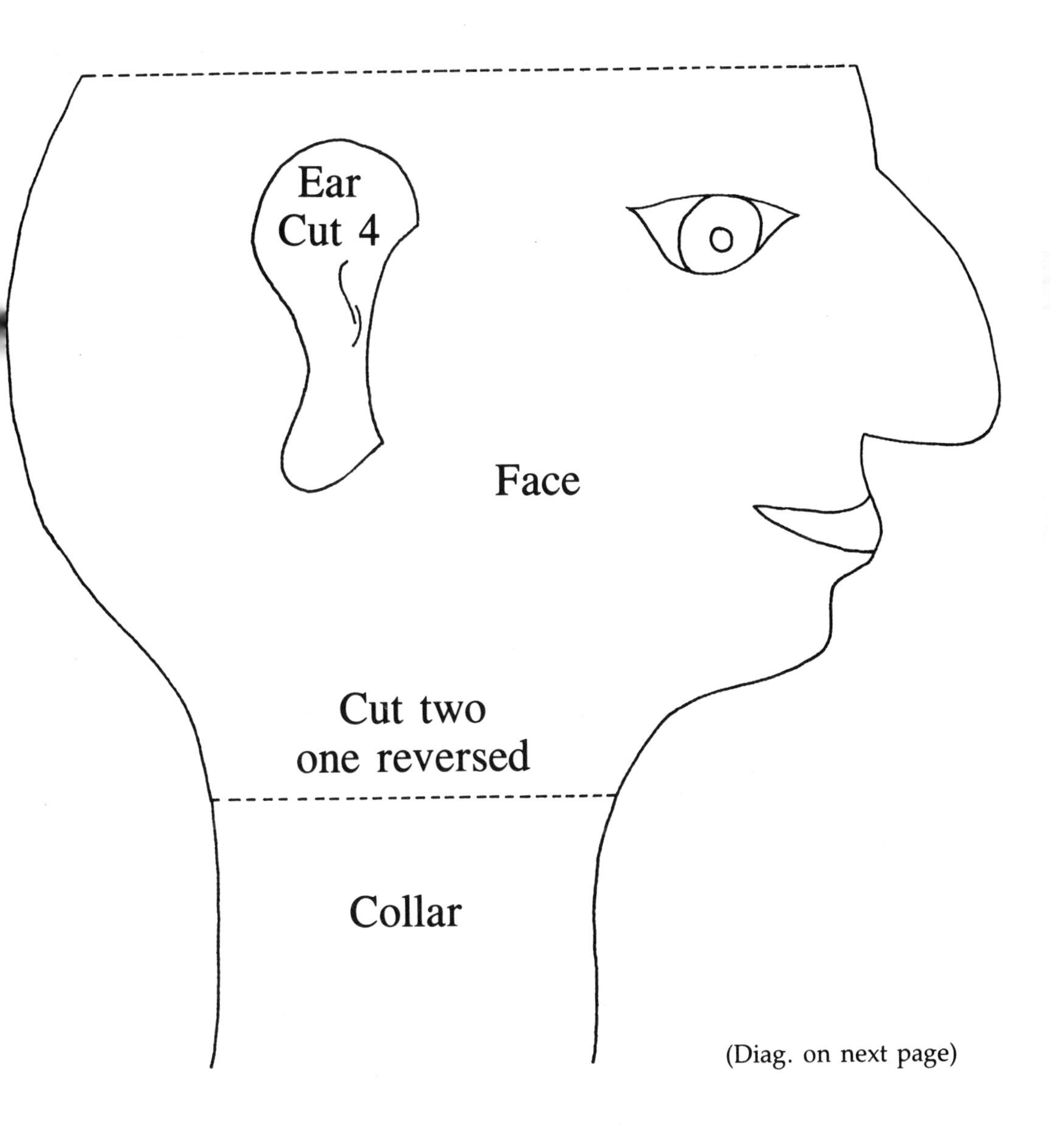

(Diag. on next page)

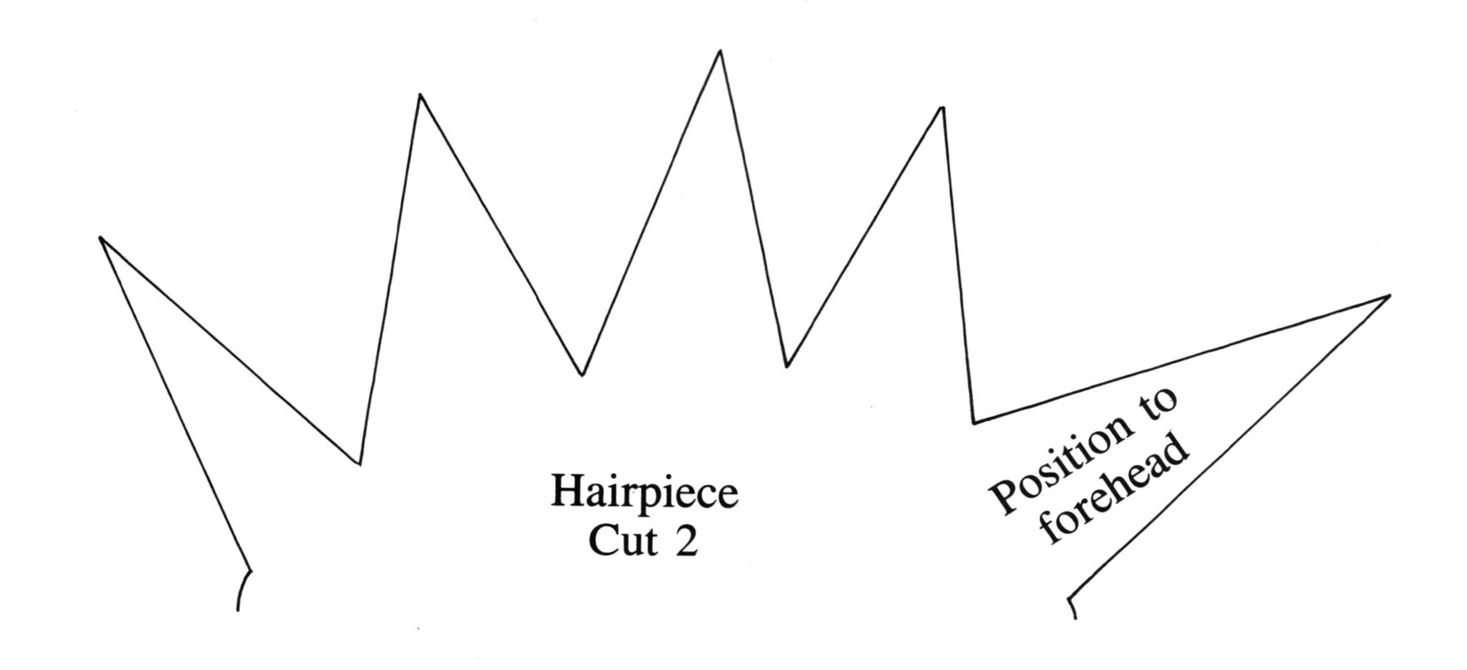
Hairpiece
Cut 2
Position to
forehead

NOVELTY

Wrist Watch

Materials

Fine canvas or evenweave in pale colour
Black fabric (approx 10cm)
Black elastic
Black and gold stranded embroidery threads

Method

1 Establish centre of watch face with pin. Using three strands of gold stranded embroidery thread, make block of four cross stitches in centre.

2 Count 10 holes outwards to each compass point and embroider two black stitches. Embroider in back stitch the hands pointing at what-ever time you wish - remember the hour hand is shorter than the minute hand!

3 Leaving two threads of canvas showing, embroider the inner rim in gold Cross stitch. Leaving one thread of canvas showing, embroider the next rim in gold back stitch, the subsequent rim in black back stitch and the final rim in black back stitch.

4 R.S together, place black backing fabric and sew, back stitch or machine, three sides and corners of fourth side. Trim excess fabric. Turn to R.S;

5 Cut a square of thick card to fit loosely inside. This is the base.

6 Stuff between the card base and the upper watch face. Sew up gap.

7 Make a bracelet of black elastic to fit just comfortably on your wrist. Join ends neatly and sew onto centre back of watch with join at the centre.

(G Ramsey)

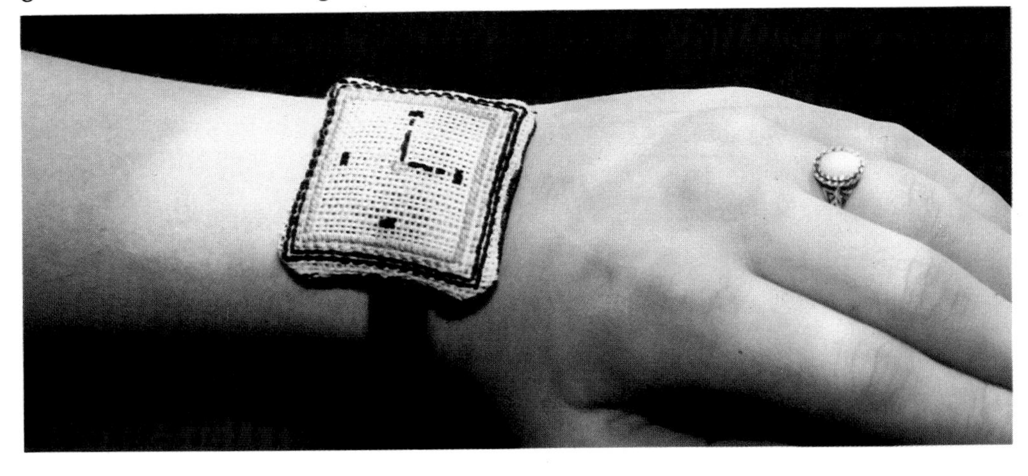

Humbugs

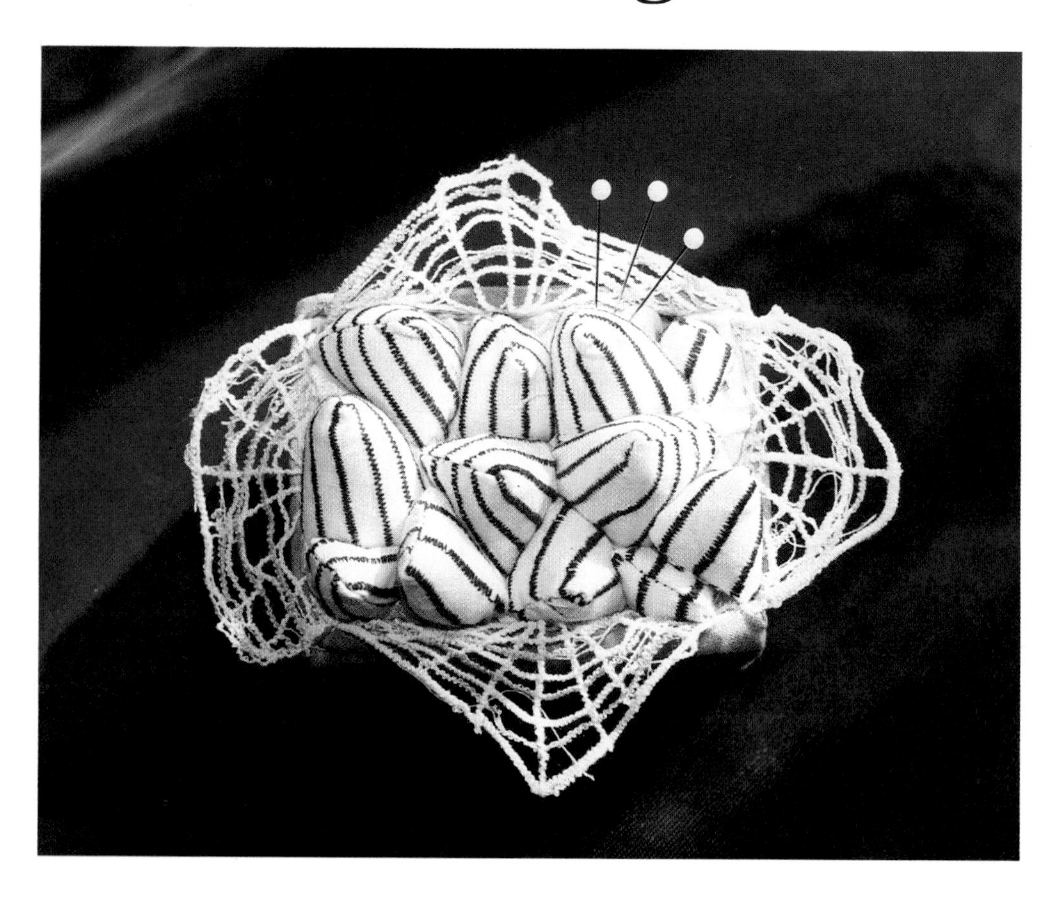

Materials

Find a small box 3½ inches x 2½ inches and about 1½ inches deep

A scrap of fabric 14 inches by 8 inches cotton or not too bulky

A scrap of white silk

Black and white striped cotton or this can be plain white and the stripes machined on using a narrow satin stitch

12 inches of lace

Terylene wadding

Method

1 Wrap your piece of fabric round the box and slip stitch tightly down one corner. Tuck in the top edge. Trim round the bottom edge but leave a flap along one side so that this can cover the bottom and then turn in the raw edges and slip stitch round the three sides.

2 Stitch the lace onto the edges of the box to make a "doily" effect.

3 Cut out a piece of white silk the size of the base and allow turnings. Cut another larger piece about 1½ inches larger on all sides, gather this larger piece and stitch to the base piece and then stab stitch at random.

4 It is now time to make the humbugs - each one takes about nine or ten stripes. Cut a strip just over an inch long fold it over and stitch one short and one long side, turn and you will have a tiny bag which can be stuffed.

5 Open the bag and centre the seam to the fold of the long side and slip stitch together. You will need seven or eight, it does not matter if each sweet is not exactly the same size or if you need more.

6 The sweets can be arranged on their silk bed, already prepared and stitched firmly.

7 Put stuffing into the box, the humbugs on top, turn any raw edges in and attach to box.

(Thelma Keller)

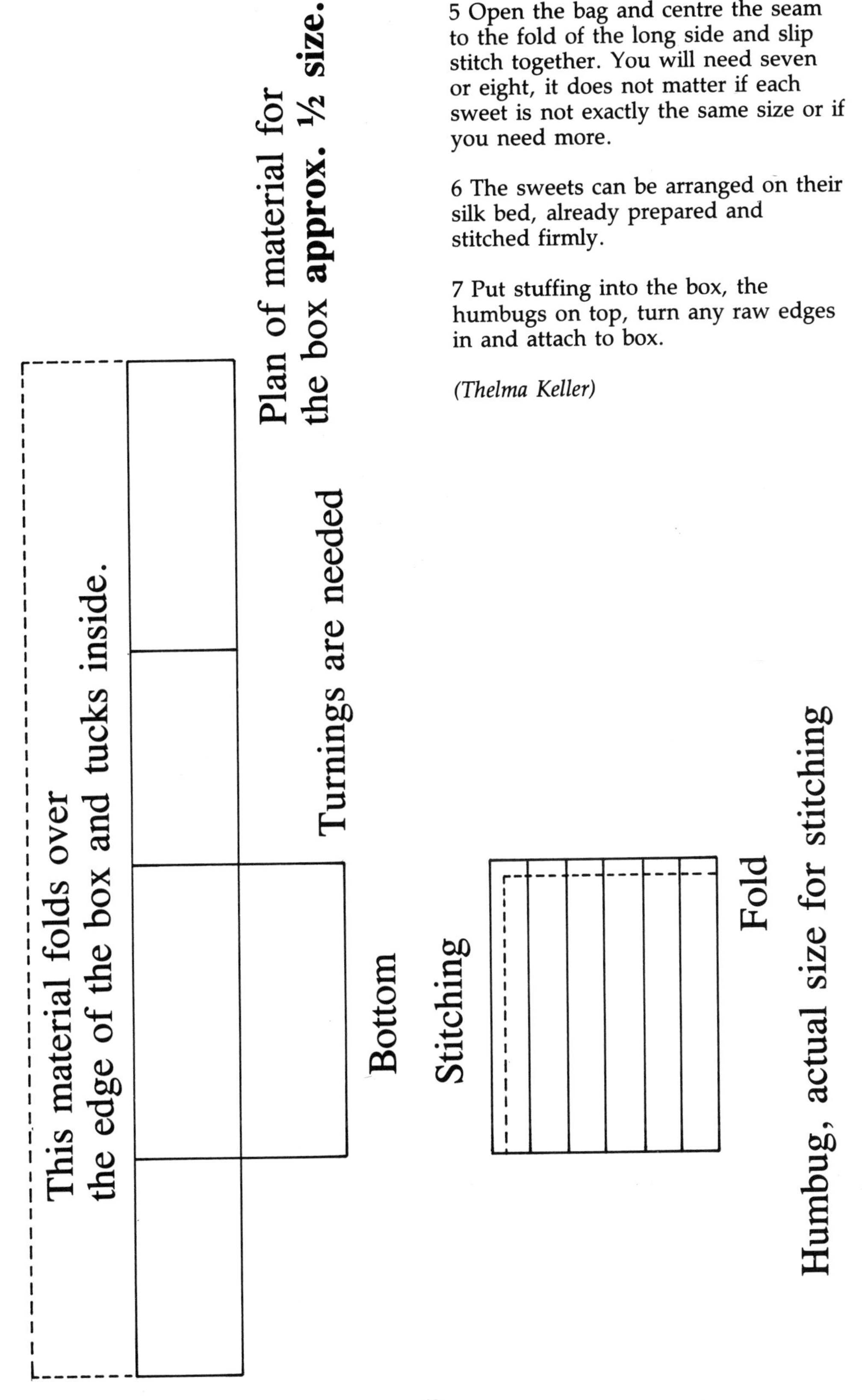

Birthday Cake

Materials

One cardboard Tube 3¼ inch diameter. (I used a tube from crochet cotton) I cut it to make a tube with a depth of 2 inches.

14 inches of a satin ribbon, 3 inches wide and the same amount of iron on vilene.

A circle of silk for the top and the same amount of wadding.

Enough white or cream ribbon to make a ruching for the top and bottom of the tube and to make a band and tie around the middle. The ribbon was ¼ inch wide.

Pink cotton.

A needleful of pink and green embroidery cotton.

A 4¼ inch diameter card circle and enough silver lame to cover.

Method

1 Iron the vilene onto the pink satin ribbon and using a fancy machine stitch, put a row of stitching along each edge about 1½ inches apart. Put this around the tube and slip stitch ends together firmly.

2 Take the circle of white silk for the top and tack the terylene wadding to it starting rom the centre. Mark on four lines to make a square and stitch these on the machine with a decorative stitch. Attach this circle to the top of the tube tucking the edges in, slip stitch round.

3 Make a tiny rose, with ribbon or embroidery (bullion knots, or straight stitches covered with blanket stitch). I found it easier to embroider when the top was on.

4 Saving enough ribbon for the tie, make your ''icing'' to go round the top and bottom by ruching the narrow white ribbon. The top ruching can be attached around the edge.

5 Cut out the card circle and cover with the lame and after stuffing the roll with shredded terylene wadding, attach the circle to the roll. You can go right through the card circle to attach and then to finish cover the base of your silver cake stand. Tie your ribbon round the cake centre.

(Thelma Keller)

(Directions for roses are on p.105)

Picture Hat

Materials
20 x 60 cm (8 x 24 in) thin white card
25 x 90 cm (10 x 36 in) Ivory Satin (or chosen colour)
2m x 50 cm (2½ yards) Single face satin ribbon (⅜″ wide)
100 cm (1¼ yards) Ivory or White lace 30mm (1¼″) deep
70 cm (¾ yard) Blue single face satin ribbon (⅜″) wide)
75 cm (⅞ yard) White lace (⅜″) deep
Dry Stick Adhesive - UHU stick
Clear Adhesive - UHU

(CF = centre front. CB = centre back)

Method
1 Cut brim patterns in white card (p.74) plus 3 x 32 cm (1⅛ x 12½″) strip for side of the crown. Curve strip into a circle the same size as the inner circle of brim, fit inside circle to measure. Glue join.

2 Using dry stick adhesive, spread evenly over the surface and cover with fabric, cover underside in the same way (card circle without hole). Snip cut out circle to **line only** (broken line on pattern), snip surplus up to line into tiny tabs (as diagram (a)). see p.74

3 Fit the prepared circle over top of brim, bring tabs up and glue round inside the side strip. Cut strip of fabric (5 x 32 cm) (2 x 12½″), join into circle, press seam open, and fit over card circle, level at bottom edge, fold surplus over the top edge, push well down, all joins at C.F. Spread glue onto brims and stick together, leave under a weight to dry.

4 Trim edge of brim by sewing 10 mm (⅜″) lace around under brim pulling lace taut so that it folds over the top brim edge (can also be glued). Fold remainder of lace over top edge of crown, pull firmly and neaten ends.

5 Fit a band of 16 mm (⅝″) ribbon around the crown joining at C.F. as before. Sew two 23 cm (9″) lace lengths to form circles, gather straight edges and pull up tightly to form rosettes.

6 Make ten roses in 10 mm (⅜″) ribbon, seven in main colour, three in chosen contrast ribbon, from 25 cm (9″) lengths. Sew three to the centre of one lace rosette and glue into place at C.F. of crown side. Sew one contrast rose to other rosette, fold 40 cm (16″) length of ribbon, sew to rosette and glue into place at C.B. of crown. Sew two main colours and one contrast rose to 3 cm (1″) strip of ribbon, trim away excess ribbon, glue onto brim edge either side of C.F.

7 Make a small cushion pad (pin cushion part) from two circles of fabric and one strip, using pattern (b), allow 10 mm (⅜″) turning. Stuff very firmly, sew up opening. Push cushion into crown, it should fit closely. Decorate top with pins, use your imagination!

(G. Bickers)

(Details for roses are on p.105)

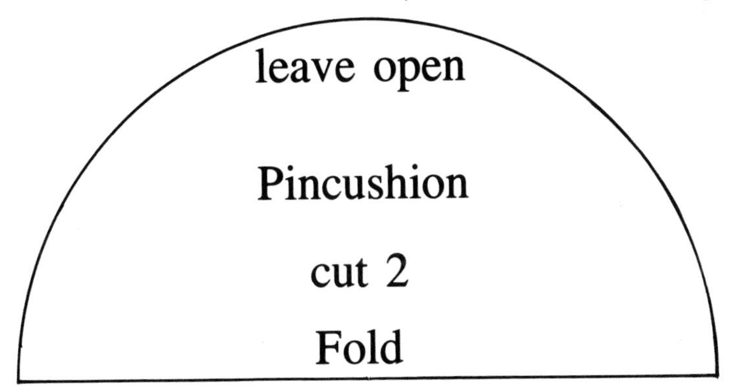

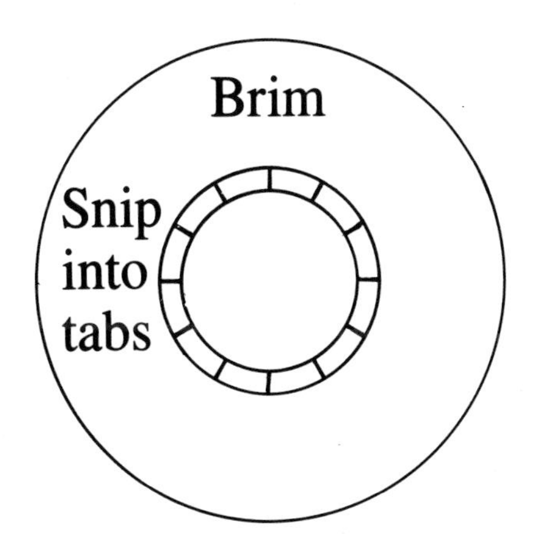

Pincushion
Strip
3 x 32cm (1½ x 12½in)

See diagram
on p.74

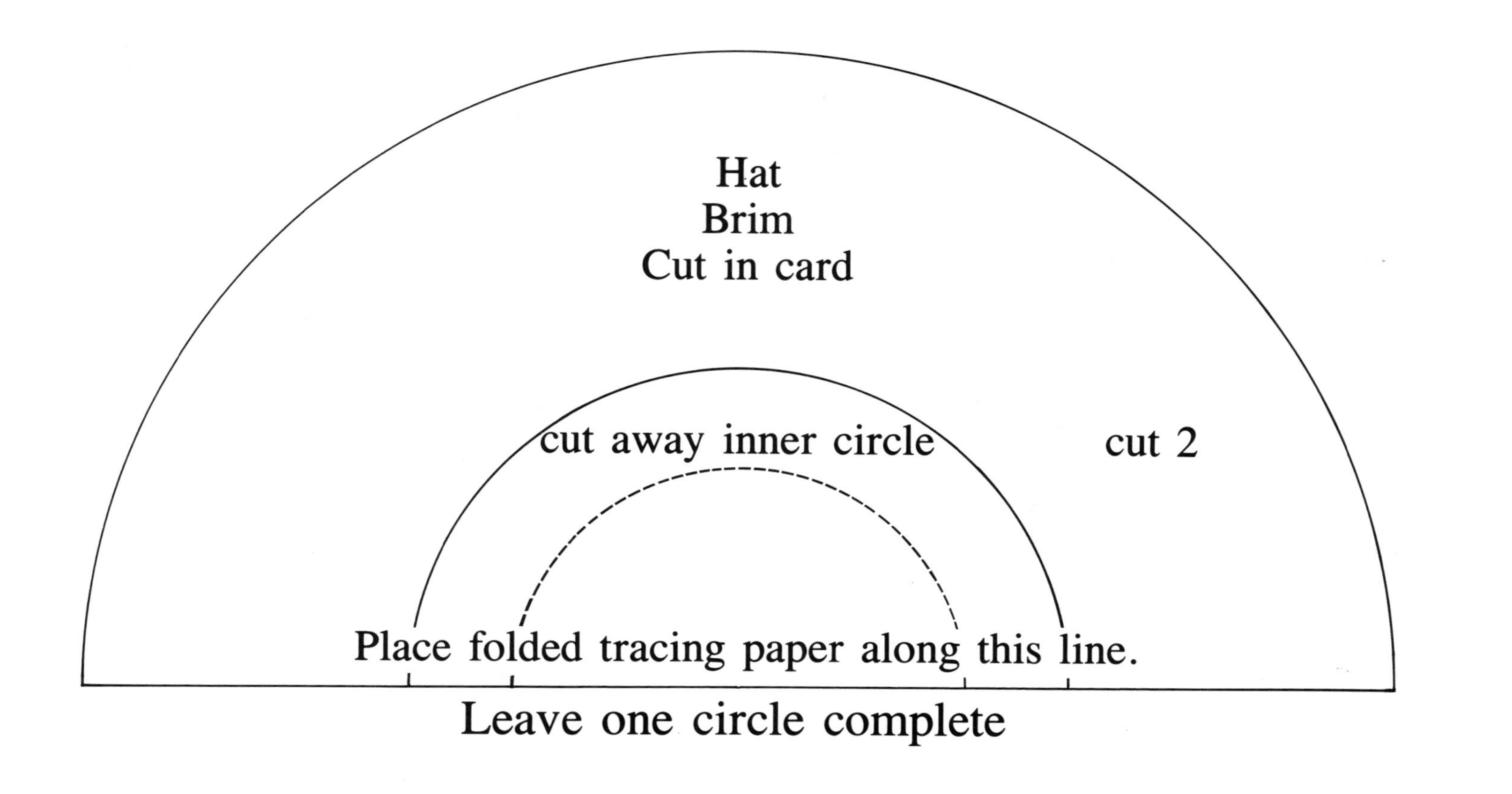
Hat
Brim
Cut in card
cut away inner circle
cut 2
Place folded tracing paper along this line.
Leave one circle complete

Cup and Saucer

Cup

1 Cut 4cm from a toilet roll tube.

2 Cut a card circle 7.5 cm diameter and another 5.5 cm diameter.

3 Cut a rectangle of material (T-shirt, polyester or cotton) 16 x 11 cm ON THE BIAS.

4 Join the short edges, right sides together, taking enough seam to make a snug fit around the cut tube.

5 Fold the fabric tube over itself, and slip the card tube into the inner half, so that it is completely covered.

6 Stitch close to lower edge of ''cup'', through both thicknesses.

7 Trim remaining fabric so 1 cm. and gather the edges through both thicknesses. Draw up, and fasten off.

Handle

1 Cut a rectangle of material 13 x 4 cms ON THE BIAS.

2 Fold, with sides to measure 6.5 x 4 cms.

3 Fold again to measure 6.5 x 2 cms, and stitch edges together, 75 mm from folded edge. Trim seam to 5 mm.

4 Turn and neaten raw edge by tucking it in. Stitch to cup.

(continued on next page).

Saucer

1 Fix a circle of wadding over 7.5 cm circle of card, with a few spots of glue.

2 Cut a circle of material 10.5 cm diameter, and gather close to the edge.

3 Place over wadded card, draw up, to fit tightly, then secure thread and fasten off.

4 Stitch the lower edge of the cup to the saucer.

5 Cut a circle of material 7.5 cm diameter, and gather close to the edge. Cover the 5.5 cm card with it. Draw up edges and fasten off.

6 Stitch it to the underside of the saucer, gathered sides together.

Tea

1 Cut a circle of pale beige stretch knit jersey-type fabric, 16 cm diameter.

2 Gather 2 cm from the edge.

3 Stuff to make an oval shape to fit cup, and draw up gathers, pushing seam up inside. Push into cup.

(Joan Perry)

Circular Garden

Materials

Approx. 4″ circle of fine brown linen for ''garden''

Approx. 3″ x 10″ of 20-1″ canvas for side ''wall''

Scrap of grey linen for ''Rock Garden''

A few metres of green crewel wool for ''Grass''

Various shades of perle cotton for flowers and leaves, etc., or use 3 strands of stranded cotton if preferred

A few metres of stone coloured perle cotton for ''wall''

A circle of card covered in green lining type material for bottom of base

(I used the empty card reel from a ball of knitting cotton for side support of ''wall'', but a ring of several layers of cardboard could be used if preferred)

Method

1 Make size of garden to fit, working embroidery as follows:

A. Satin St. Blocks (Beige).
B. Apply scraps of grey linen and decorate with French Knots in yellow and white.
C. French Knots in orange, straight st. in green.
D. Straight st. in blue, detached chain in green.
E. Bullion knots in purple, straight st. in green.
F. Large French Knots in pink, detached chain in green.
G. French Knots in lavender, straight st. in green.
H. French Knots in red, straight st. in yellow, and straight st. in green.

(continued on next page).

2 Work "wall" on canvas with Tent St. in stone coloured perle to the depth of 1½", then decorate with stem st. and French Knots to form a trailing effect. Work remaining ½" in velvet st. in green crewel wool to represent "grass". Do not cut loops until rest of pincushion is finished.

3 Fit embroidered "wall" around reel and tuck raw edges inside reel top and bottom; stick down inside or lace firmly if preferred.

4 Fit embroidered "garden" with excess material tucked inside top of reel and secure with strong neat stitches.

5 Stuff pincushion firmly through bottom of reel. Do not use cotton wool as this would attract dampness and damage pins. The best stuffing is sheep's wool if you are a spinner, or emery powder, if obtainable; but terylene wadding is suitable. I always put a small dressmaker's weight into the centre of the stuffing to give firmness. Cover in the bottom with the green covered card disc, stitched neatly but strongly; and, last of all, cut and trim the "grass".

(Olive Caselton)

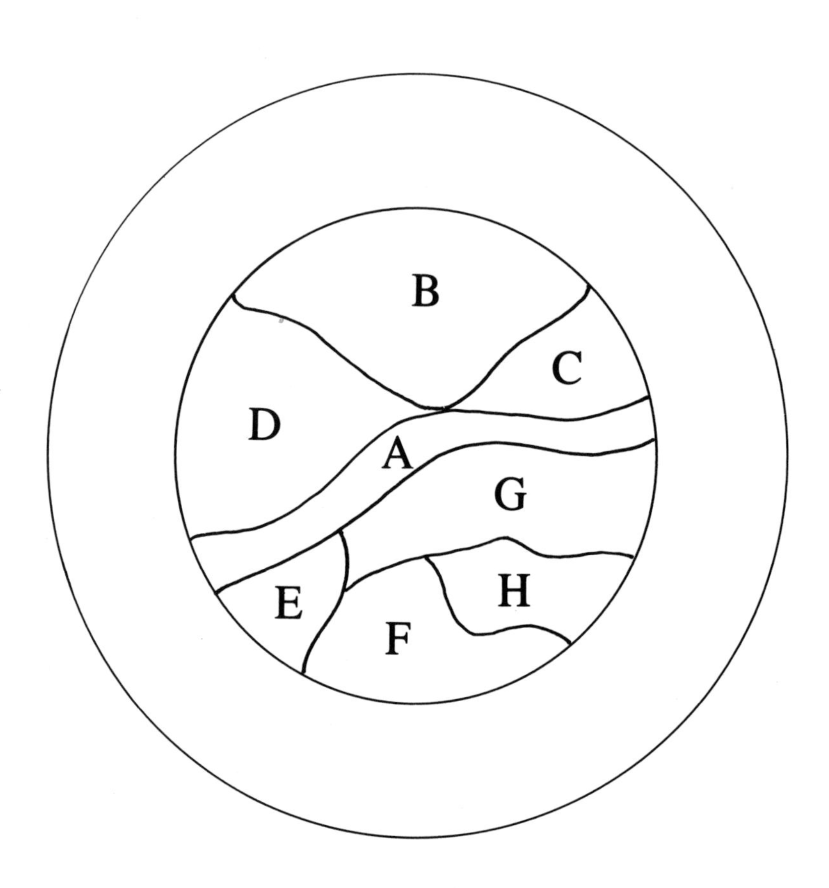

Teapot

This pin cushion can be made into a thimble-holder if the cardboards are left in the 8 pieces, a "bag" lining attached and the lid attached at one point only.

Materials
Cut 8 pieces of thin card as pattern
Cut 8 pieces of fabric, 4 plain, 4 patterned, preferably allowing ¼" turnings to cover

Method

Teapot:
1 Cover each cardboard template with fabric, but **do not** take tacking through front fabric, just lace over back. This is because the cardboard will be removed later.

2 Embroider the plain pieces if desired.

Oversew these 8 sections together on wrong side, then turn to right side.

3 Cover a small measured octagonal piece of cardboard and sew onto teapot as base.

4 With a small pair of sharp scissors, cut through tackings on wrong sides of the 8 pieces and withdraw the cardboard.

5 Stuff firmly.

6 Make a LID by covering a circle of cardboard and padding out slightly.

(continued on next page).

7 Add appropriate sized bead for a knob, and small beads can be sewn around if liked.

8 Attach to the tea-pot body.

Handle:
1 Wind a narrow cross-way strip of fabric around two lengths of pipecleaner.

2 Wrap around with "cotton."

3 Cut to length required after "fitting" allowing ¼" turning at top and bottom.

4 Attach to pot.

Spout:
1 Cut out cardboard spout to shape.

2 Cover, pad a little, and attach.

(Joan Appleton Fisher)

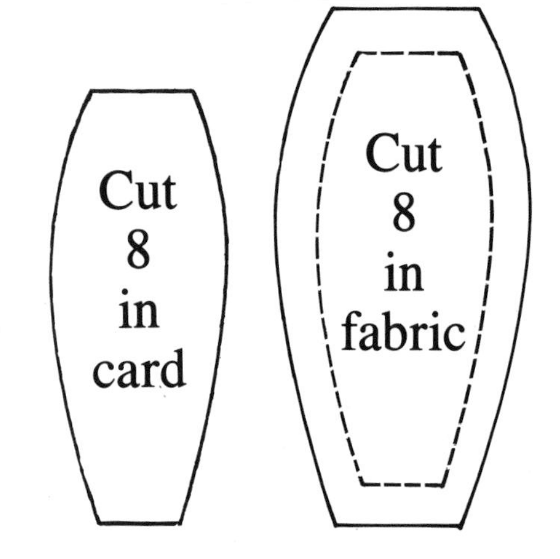

The Garden Next Door

Materials
Six squares of card
Six squares of dupion (I used blue) large enough to lace onto the card squares
Small amount of calico
One card hexagon and material to cover for the base
Three shades of green cotton
Various shades of yellow, blue, pink, orange, red, grey, stranded cotton for the embroidery

Method
1 Put your chosen material onto a frame and draw round your card square six times, remember when cutting them out to leave turnings.

2 Put in a few straight lines as guide lines for the embroidery and then start to embroider free flower shapes in various colours. Simple stitches such as lazy daisy, blanket stitch, french knots, can be used.

3 When completed cut out and stretch onto the square shapes and join them up to make a hexagon shape.

4 Mark out a hexagon shape on a piece of calico for the top, this is the lawn. Stripes in two shapes of green can either be worked by hand using stem stitch or as I did be worked on the sewing machine using a zig zag stitch. Round the edge I made a tiny hedge using the Tailor tack foot. This shape can now be fitted into the hexagon and sewn round the edge.

5 Using calico in a frame make six irregular slips for the corners and one circular one for the centre. Use textured stitches, knots, blanket stitch, detached button hole stitch, carry through with the same colours. Attach these to the centre and at the points.

6 Lastly cover the hexagon for the bottom and after stuffing the main shape with shredded terylene using ladder stitch fix the bottom to the sides.

(Thelma Keller)

(continued on next page).

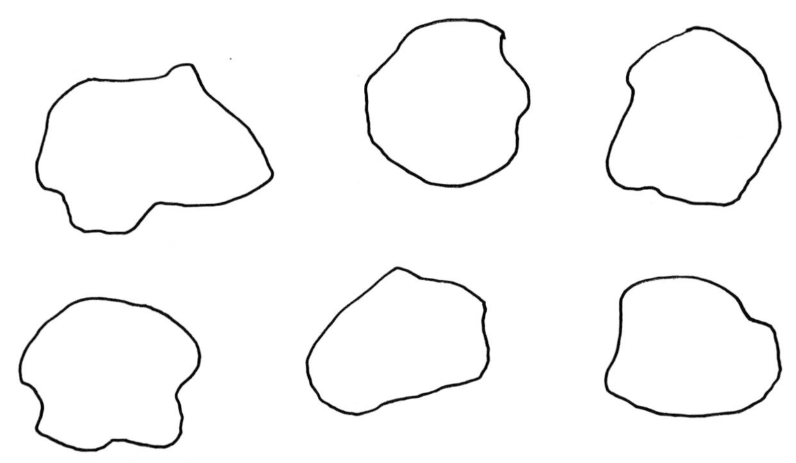

six irregular slips for corners.

One card hexagon covered for base. One calico hexagon embroidered for lawn.

Six squares of card and six pieces of material slightly larger.

20
1
18
4
13
6
10
15
2
17
3
19
7
16
8
11
14
9
12
5

Dartboard

Materials

1 strip black cotton 2 inches wide by 23 inches
2 ten inch squares black cotton fabric
1 ten inch square white polycotton fabric
1 ten inch square 2 oz polyester wadding
1 ten inch square cream cotton fabric
1 ten inch square green cotton fabric
1 ten inch square red cotton fabric
Black, red, green and cream thread
Metallic silver thread
Stuffing

Method

1 Trace the design onto the white polycotton with a pencil.

2 Make a sandwich with the black cotton, wadding and white polycotton, pin and tack together through all layers.

3 Pin the cream cotton over the black cotton and working from the wrong side, (the white polycotton) machine stitch round the cream areas on the design.

4 Turn work to right side, trim round stitching as close as possible leaving the cream areas appliqued over the black.

5 With a close zig-zag stitch go round the cream areas covering all the edges. Work the green and red areas in the same way.

6 Using the silver metallic thread, embroider the numbers and edge all the colours using back stitch.

7 Join the short ends of the strip of black cotton, right sides together, taking a ½″ seam.

8 Following the outer edge of the design, stitch the strip round the circle right sides together. Trim round seam.

9 Cut a circle out of the second square of black cotton using the outer edge of the design as a pattern.

10 Right sides together, stitch onto other long side of the strip leaving an opening.

11 Turn the work to the right side, fill with stuffing and stitch the opening together.

(Heather Aldridge)

(Diagrams on next pages).

20
5
12
9
14
11
8
16
7
19

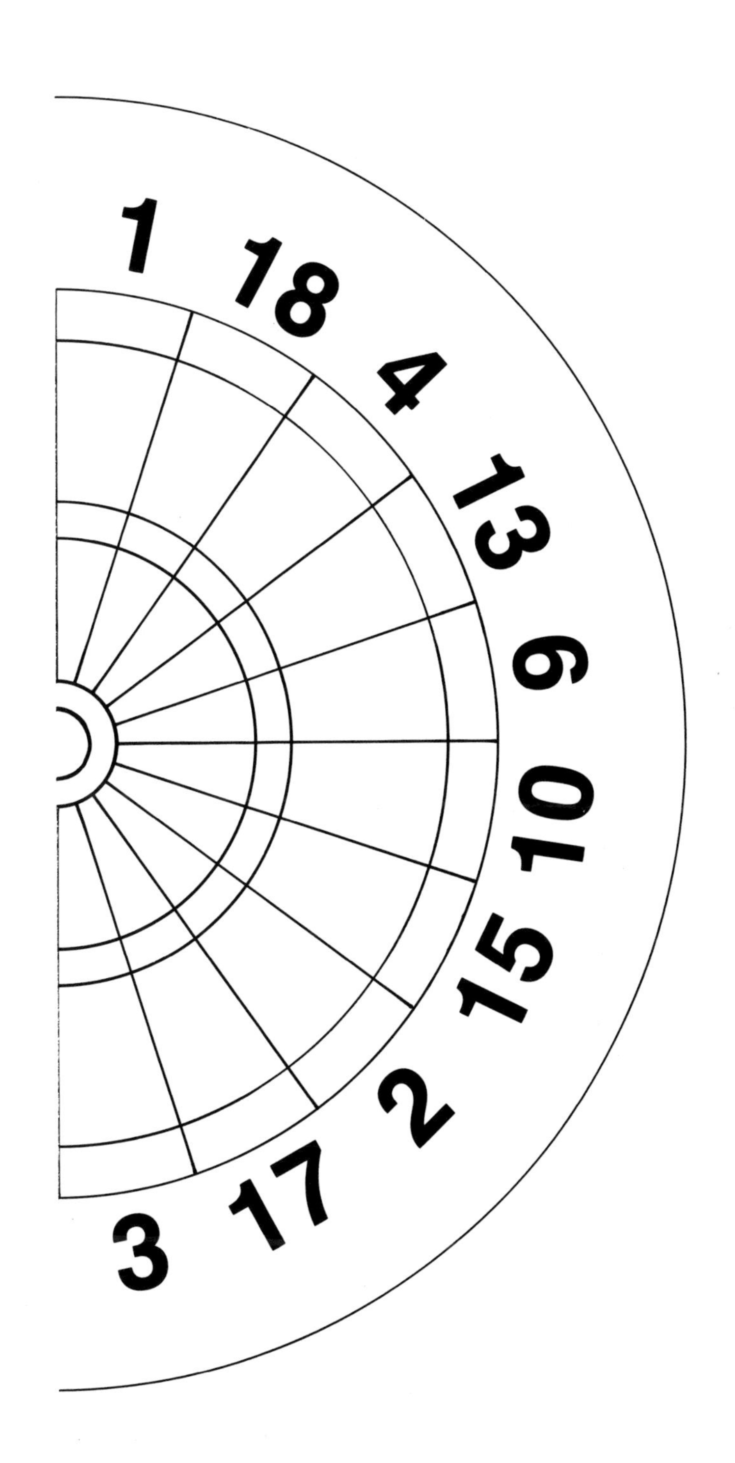
1
18
4
13
6
10
15
2
17
3

M·I·S·C·E·L·L·A·N·E·O·U·S

Pin and Thread Holder

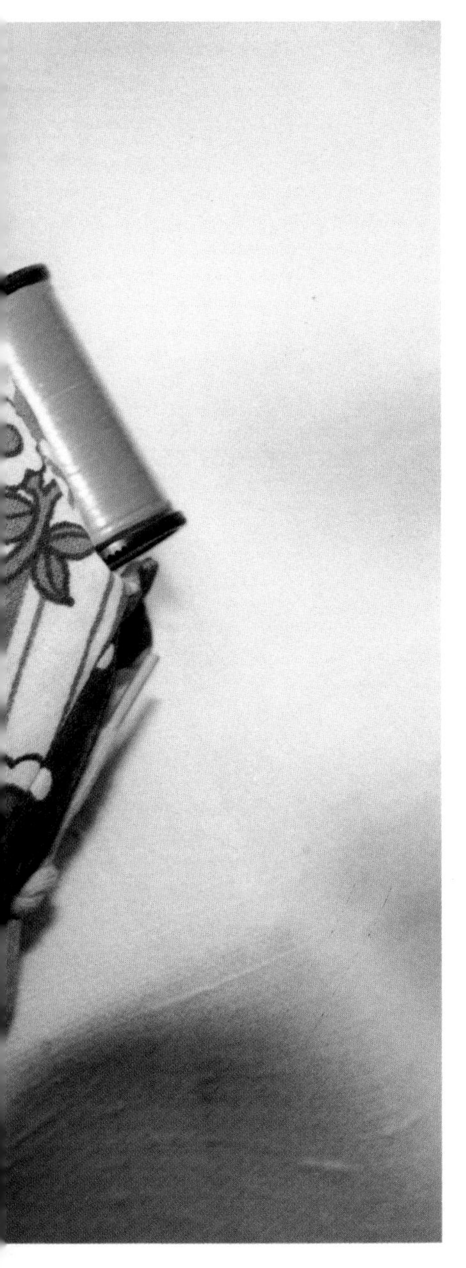

This is a traditional design used by Durham quilters.

For the top and bottom, I used two 2½ inch hexagons, leaving the card template in the bottom one. Six long hexagons were used for the side pieces - the ends fit together, which are then fixed with eyelets, for a cord to pass through. I used a shoe lace, as the metal end makes it easy to thread through the cotton reels.

(Rose Bell)

Braid Humbug

I made this pincushion with braid (1.5 cm wide) woven on an inkle loom. Six strips were stitched together to create the stripes. The side seams were joined together, then stuffing added, carefully moulding the shape. The remaining seams were closed, and then a loop of handmade Japanese braid was added, in matching colours.

(Jean Thornton)

Tenerife Lace

Materials
Approx 3″ diameter smooth lid (eg. Nivea no. 2)
3 pieces approx 5″ square fabric
1 skein coton à broder or similar to tone with fabric
5″ square of cardboard - firm but flexible

Method
1 Draw 3″ circle on cardboard and mark 32 equal segments on outer edge.

2 With strong thread, back stitch round edge on marks. Fasten off with knot.

3 With a long piece of coton à broder, weave across the circle edge to edge through the back stitches to form a web. DO NOT attach the coton à broder to the card at any point.

The centre crossing threads are secured by weaving under and over to form a centre for the lace, ending with a row of knots. This weaving and flat knot stitch form the patterns in teneriffe lace. When the lace pattern is finished, knot adjacent loops together so that the knots can't slip off. Snip the back stitches on the card to release the lace.

Making up
Cover the lid outside with a circle of fabric, sticking the edge inside. Cut a further two circles of fabric and machine R.S. together, leaving space for turning through. Stuff firmly. Close opening with ladder stitch. Push into box lid and sew top edge to covered lid with tiny stitches. Carefully centre lace circle onto padded top, pin in place and catch stitch top of each loop onto padded surface.

(G Ramsey)

Celtic Cross

This pincushion has been designed from the Celtic Cross at Carew in Pembrokeshire. I have used Italian quilting to raise the Celtic knot design.

Materials

2 squares of woollen fabric, 15 cm x 15 cm each
1 square of cotton, 15 cm x 15 cm
1 skein coton a broder in chosen colour
1 skein stranded cotton in the same colour
A small amount of stuffing
Quilting wool
Tracing paper

Method

1 Trace over pattern on to tracing paper.

2 Tack together tracing paper on top of 1 square of woollen fabric on top of cotton fabric.

3 With small stitches, tack along all the lines of the pattern through all three layers.

4 Tear tracing paper away. Your design should now be tacked on to your fabric.

5 With back stitch, sew along the two outside lines of the pattern using coton a broder. Make sure you sew through both layers of material.

6 With 3 strands of stranded cotton and back stitch, sew along the middle line of the pattern.

7 Take out all tacking stitches.

8 With a large-eyed needle, thread the quilting wool in between the two layers. Do not cross over the bars but start each bar separately.

9 Push in all loose ends and sew over the holes.

10 Place 2nd square of woollen fabric over the pattern and sew together leaving 1 cm between seam and pattern all round. Leave an opening along one side.

11 Trim seams and clip curves. Turn right side out.

12 Stuff the pin cushion firmly and sew up the opening.

(Pam Canning)

Diagram on next page.

Celtic Cross diagram.

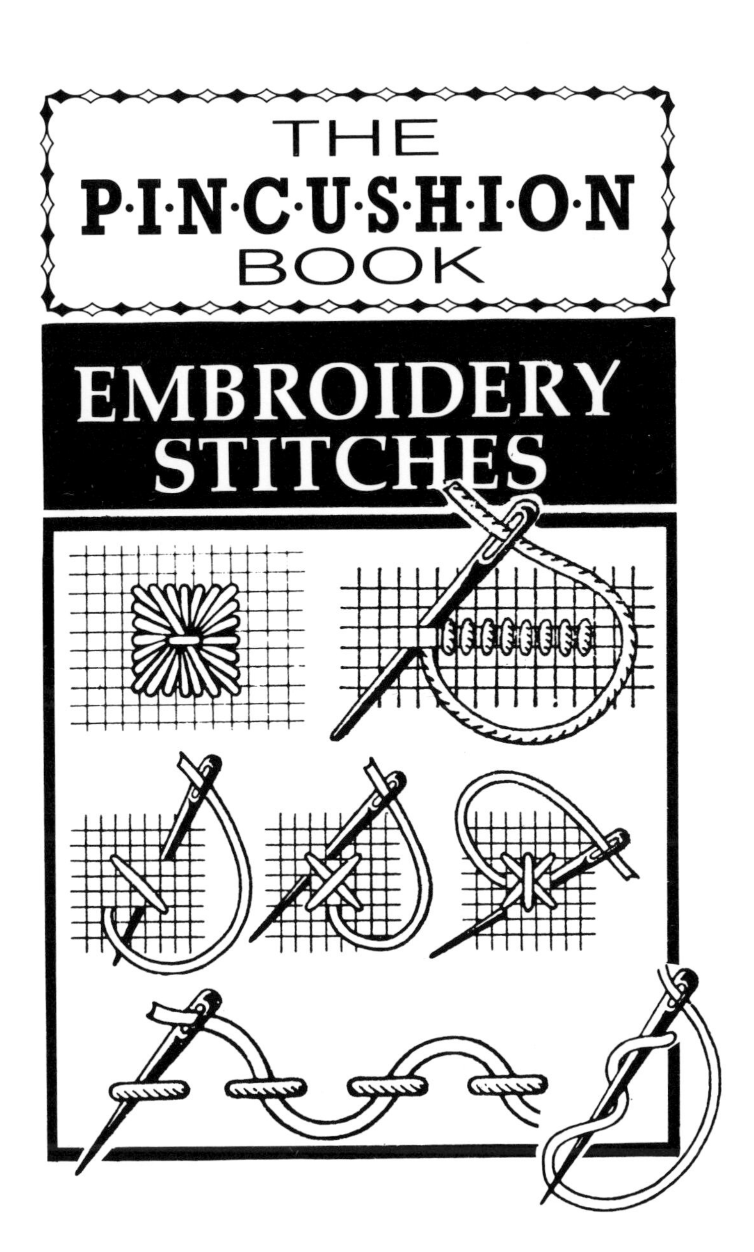
THE
P·I·N·C·U·S·H·I·O·N
BOOK
EMBROIDERY
STITCHES

Algerian Eye Stitch

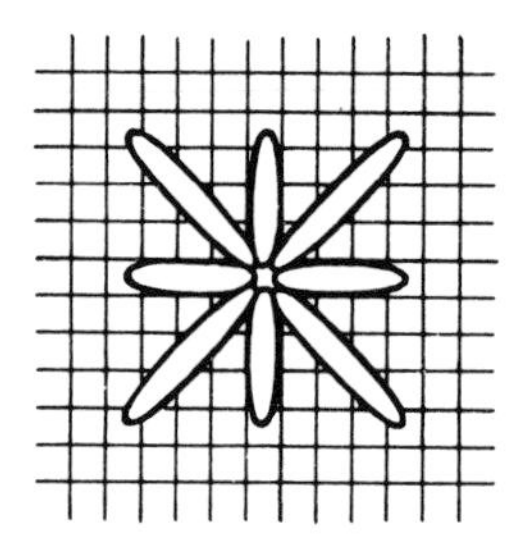

Back Stitch

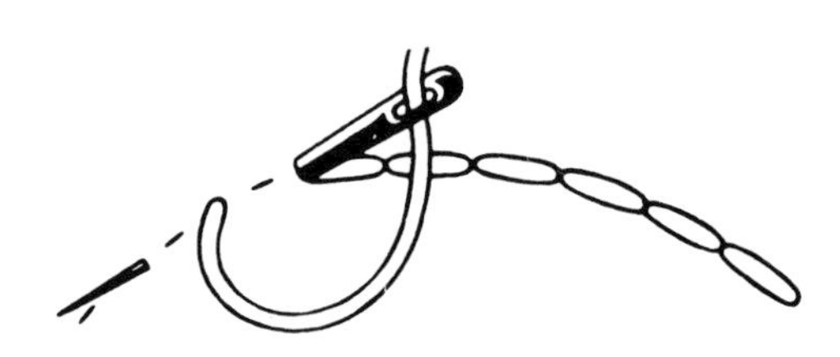

Blanket Stitch

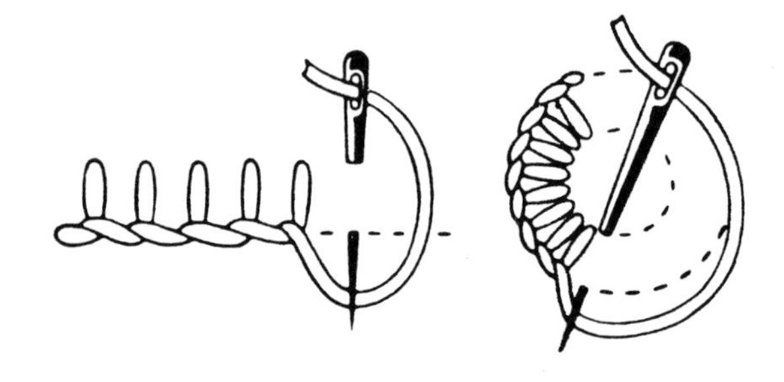

Brick Stitch
(also Long and Short Stitch)

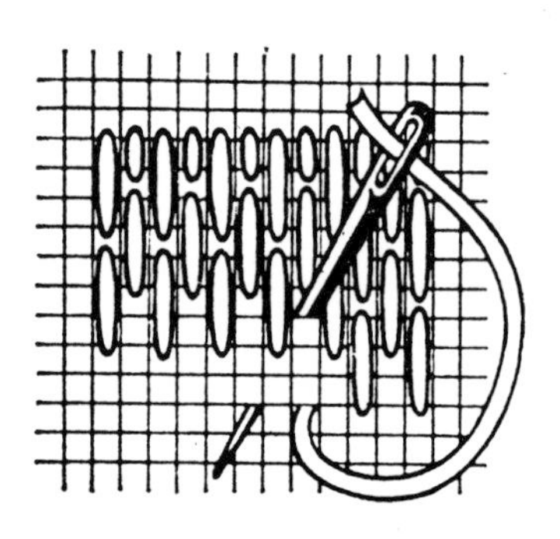

Bullion Stitch

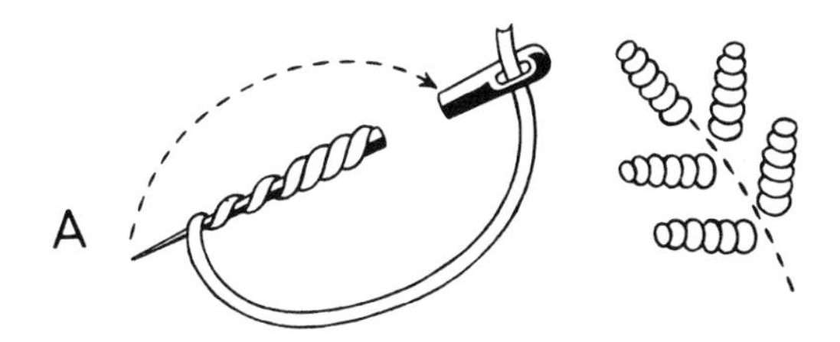

Chain Stitch

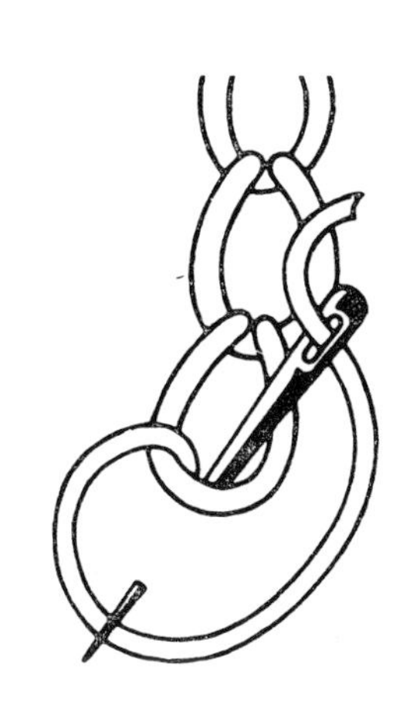

Couching

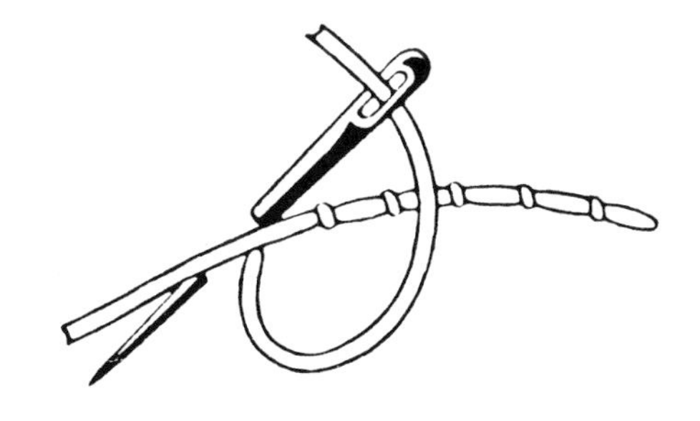

Cretan Stitch

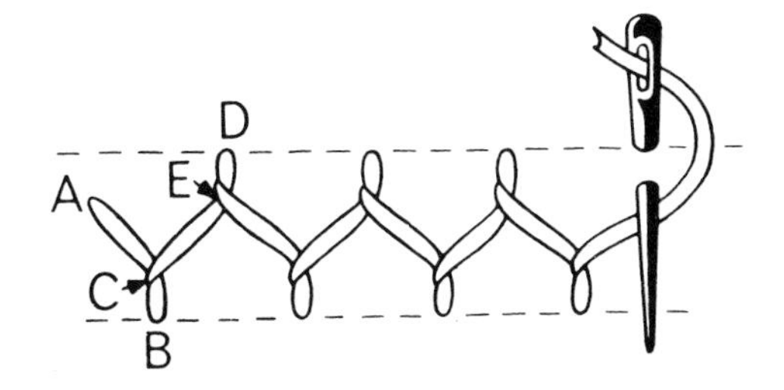

Cross Stitch

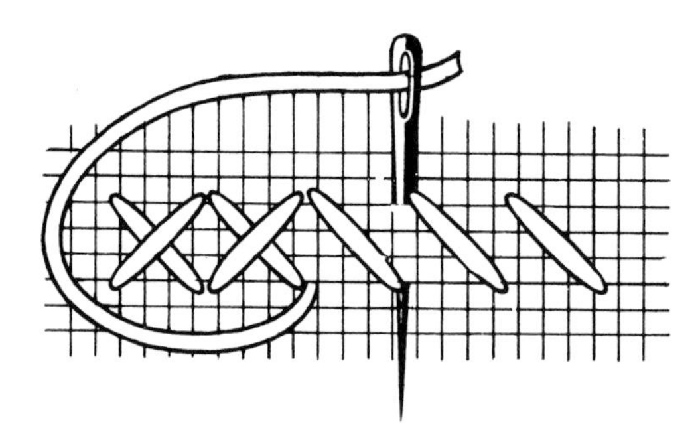

Cushion Stitch (A) (alternated with Tent Stitch (B))

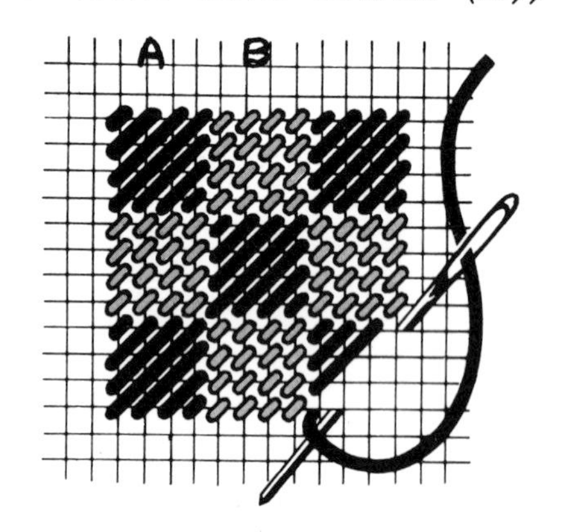

Double Cross Stitch

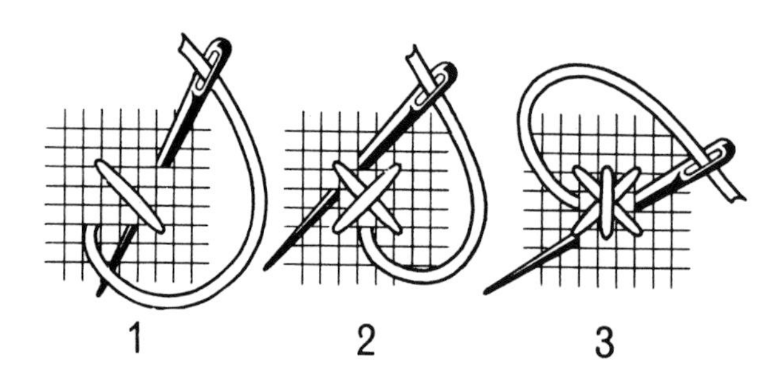

Feather Stitch

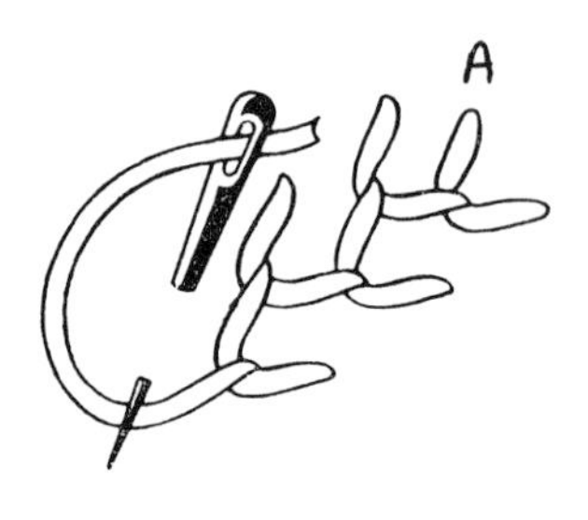

Fly Stitch

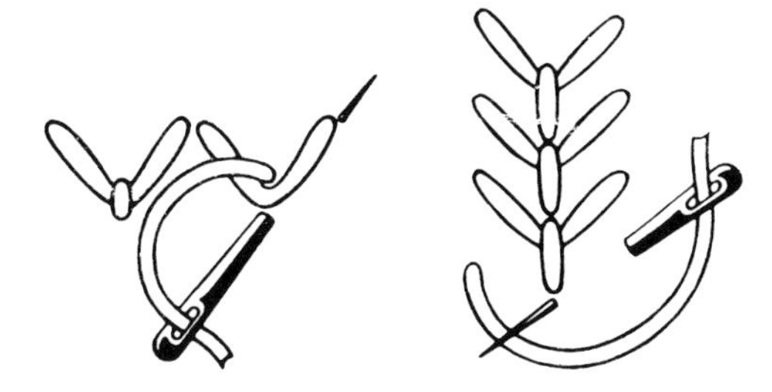

French Knots

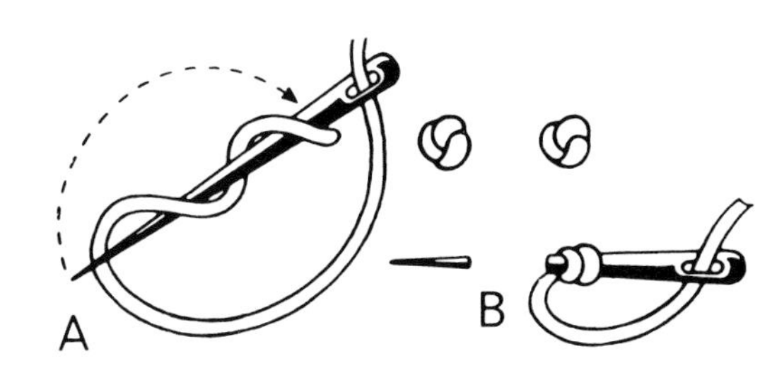

Gobelin Stitch

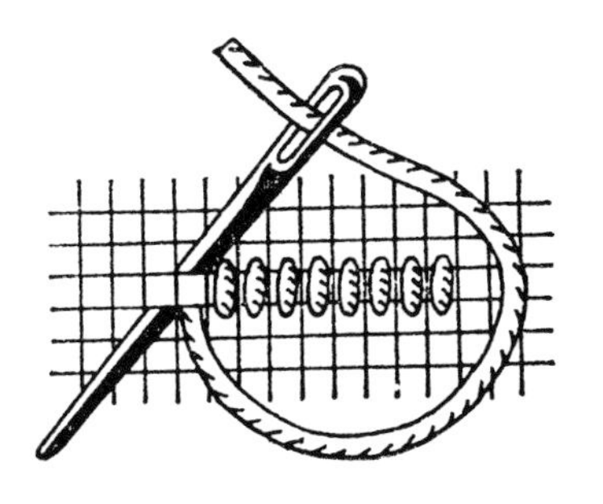

Leaf Stitch

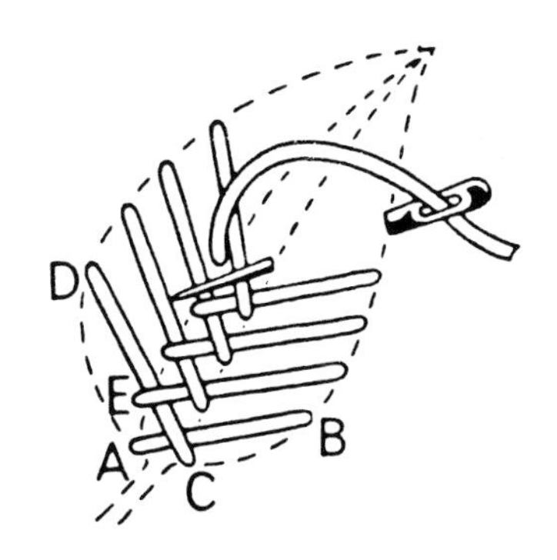

Long and Short Stitch
(see Brick Stitch)

Long-Armed Cross Stitch

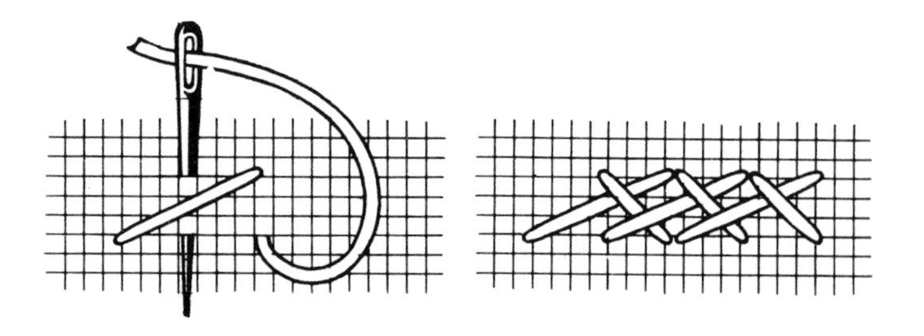

Mosaic Filling

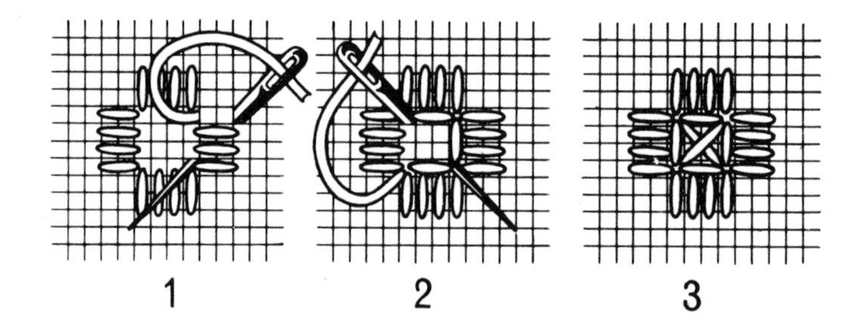

Rhodes Stitch

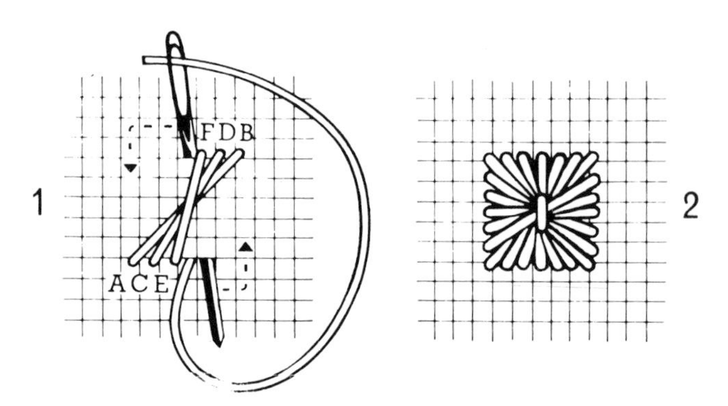

Running Stitch

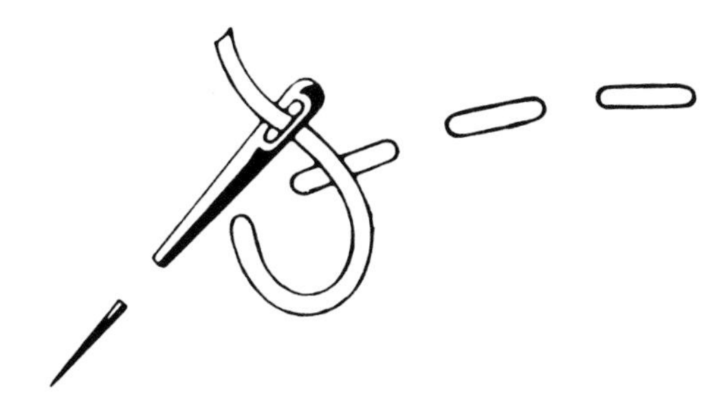

Running Stitch (Laced)

Satin Stitch

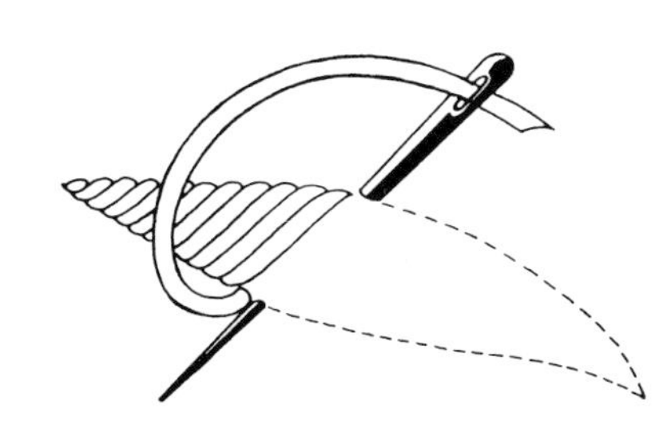

Spider's Web

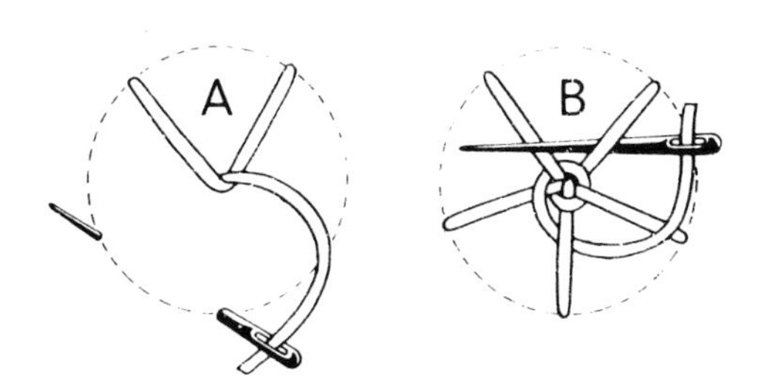

Stem Stitch

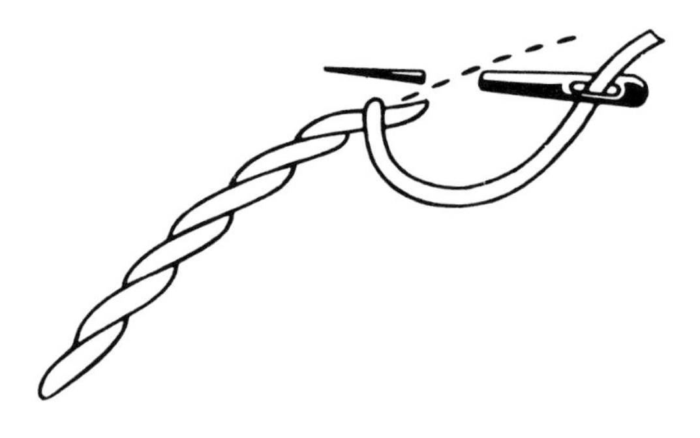

Tent Stitch

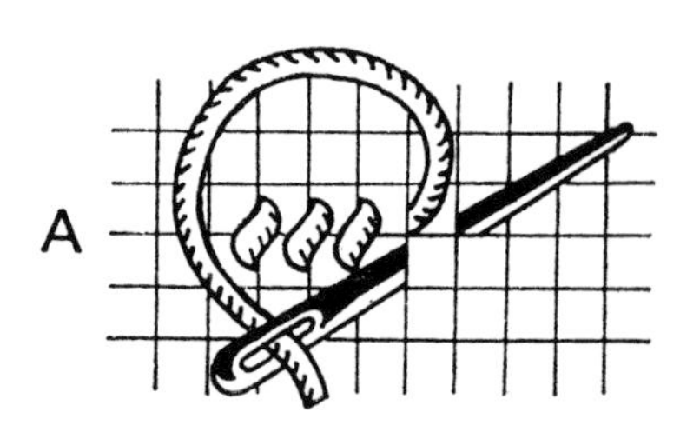

B

Velvet Stitch

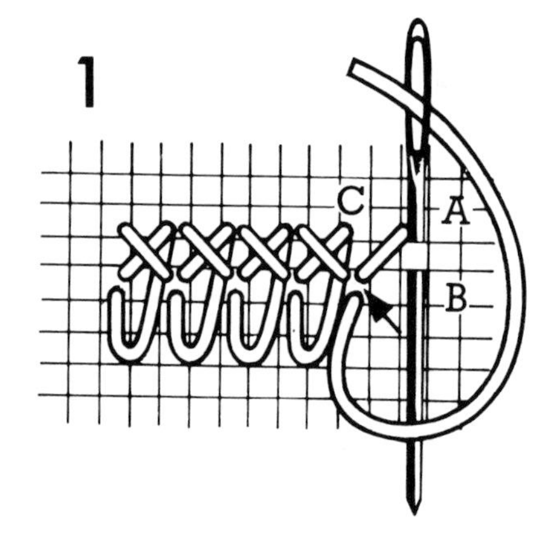

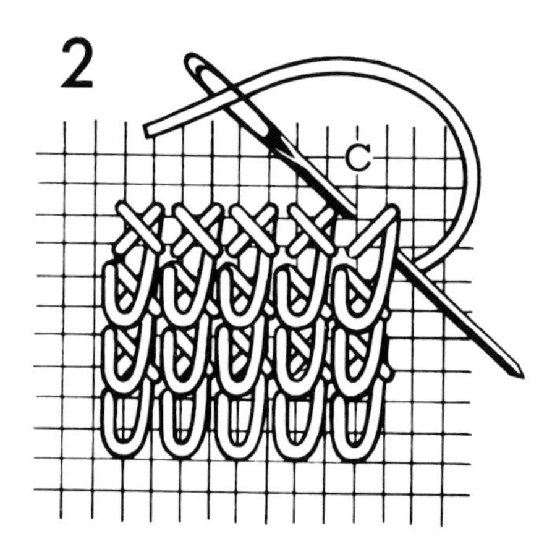

Ribbon Roses

For each rose you will need ½ metre of satin ribbon; (the size of the finished rose depends on the ribbon width used). Tight winding creates buds, looser winding makes full-blown roses and narrow ribbons (such as 9mm wide) form rosettes.

Method

1 To form the centre roll one end of ribbon six turns to make a tight tube. Sew a few stitches at base to secure. (Diag. 1).

2 To form petals, fold top edge of unwound ribbon downward and toward you so it is parallel to tube and folded edge is at a 45° angle. (Diag. 2).

3 Roll tube across fold and angled down; roll and tack, shaping the rose as you work, until it is desired size. Finish by turning under raw edge and sewing to base. (Diag. 3).

Use Offray ribbons.

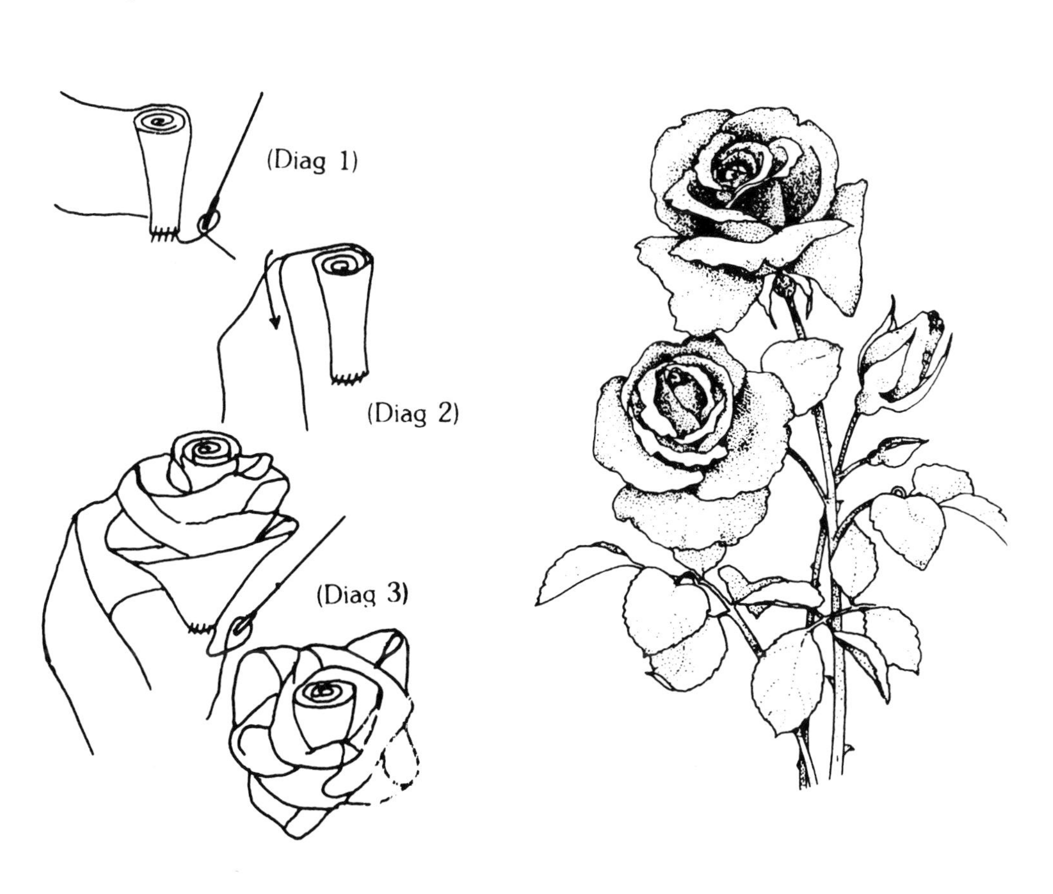

Floral Motifs

Patchwork Shapes

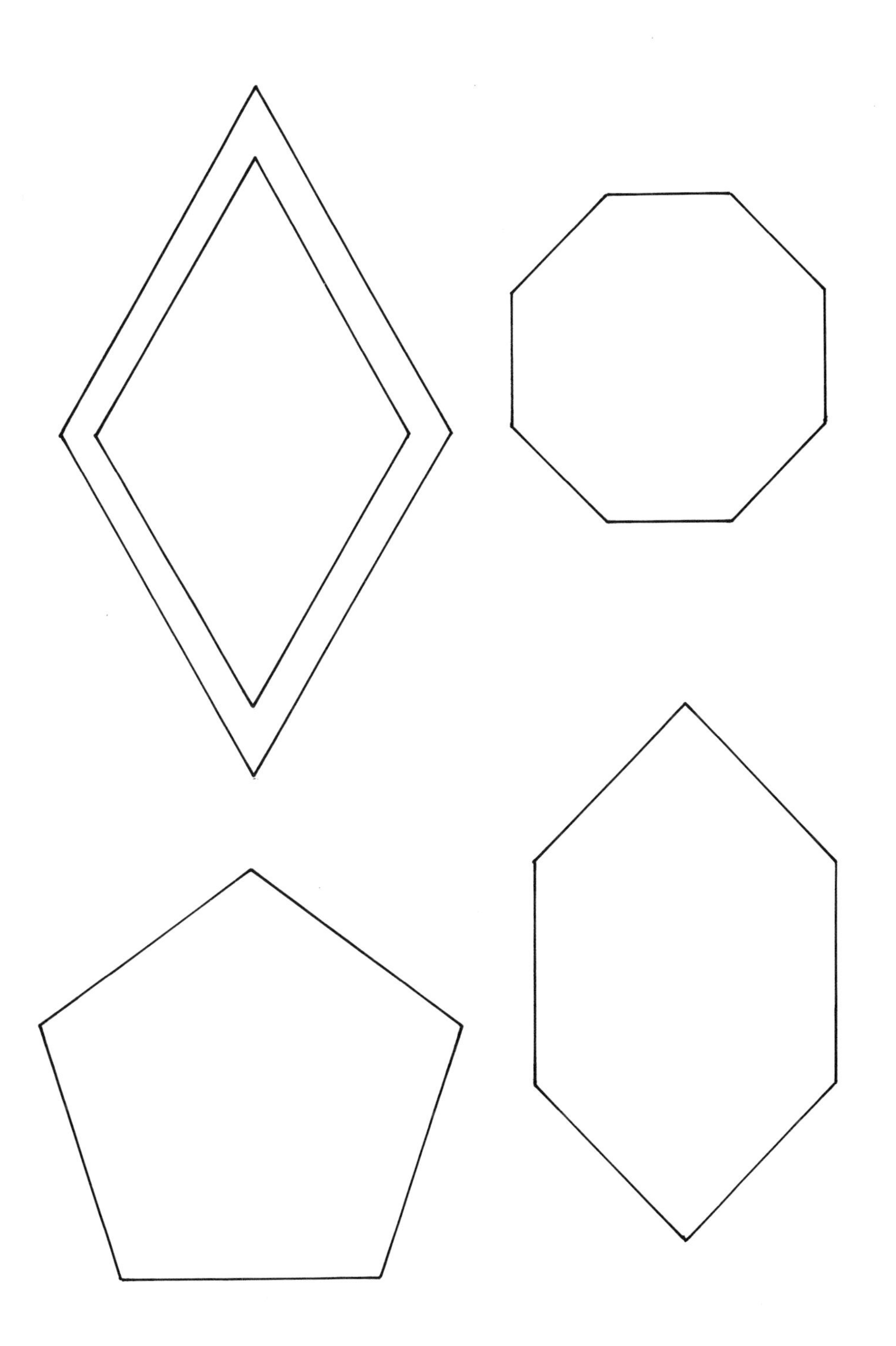

Alphabet

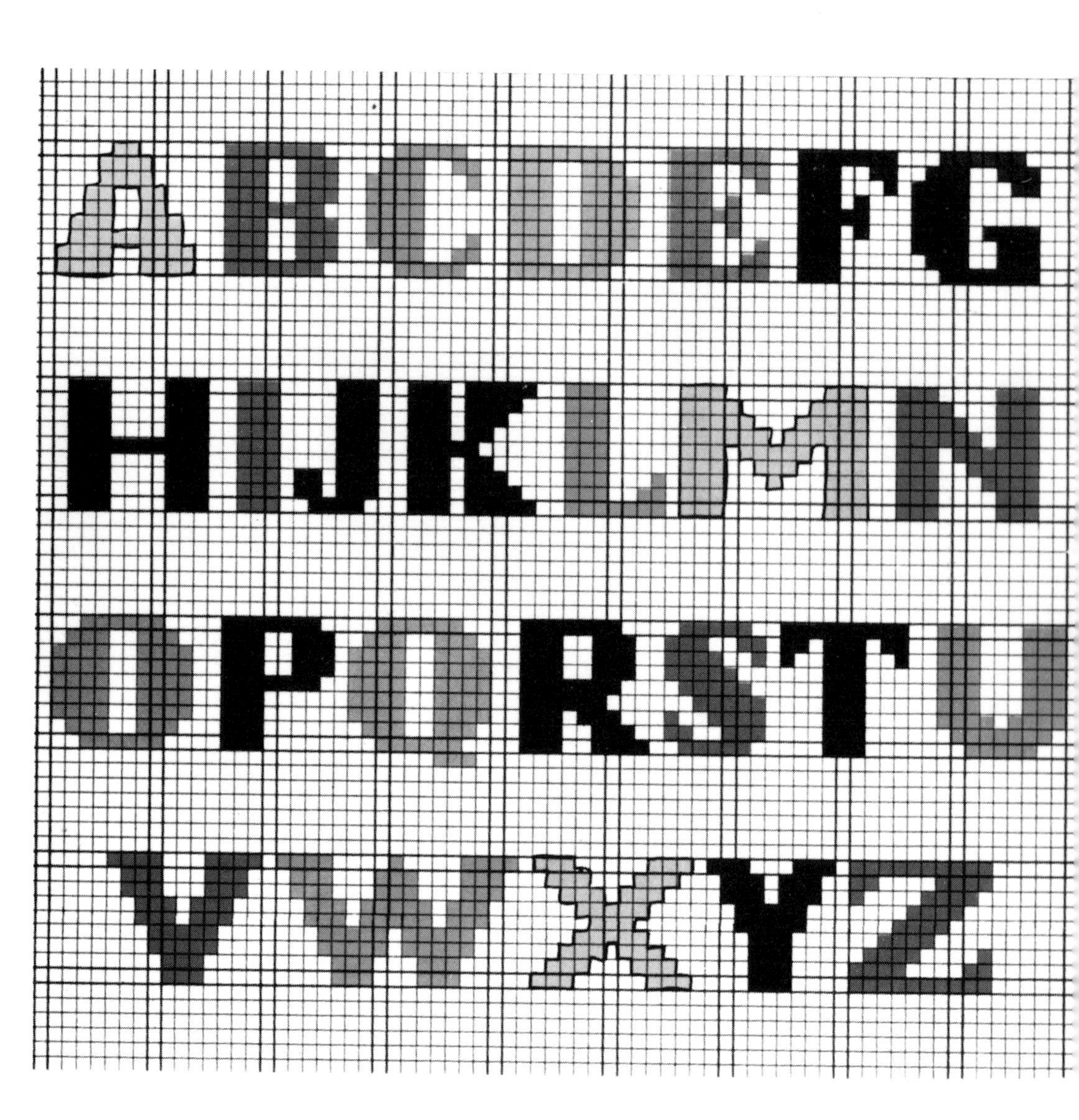

National Needle Museum

Forge Mill Museum has been established to preserve items from the needle and fishing tackle industries of Redditch and to display them in an interesting and colourful manner.

The River Arrow, providing a source of power to drive the machinery of the needle scouring (polishing) and pointing mills had, in earlier days, encouraged monks of the Cistercian order to build Bordesley Abbey close to its banks.

Both Museum and Abbey are set in beautiful open meadowland, some 100 acres in all, offering pleasant country walks and superb picnic areas.

An informative guided tour is recommended — it's available seven days a week. Evening bookings are also taken but only on Tuesday, Wednesday and Thursday.

Life-like models enhance display areas and the guided tour will bring this unique museum to life as you follow the history of needlemaking. As well as explaining the history, the Museum shows some of the many uses to which needles are put.

Embroidery exhibitions and demonstrations are also arranged.

OPEN

April to October

Weekdays	11.00 a.m. to 4.30 p.m.
Saturday	1.00 p.m. to 5.00 p.m.
Sundays & Bank Holidays	11.30 a.m. to 5.00 p.m.

November to March

Weekdays only	11.00 a.m. to 4.30 p.m.

Parties welcome at any time but **prior notification** is necessary (reduced rates).
Wheelchairs can be accommodated in the Museum with the exception of the top floor.

FURTHER DETAILS FROM

Forge Mill National Needle Museum, Needle Mill Lane, Riverside, Redditch, Worcs. B97 6RR. (Tel: 0527 62509).

All the pincushions in this book will be on permanent display at the Museum.

A Pin For Every Occasion

Dorcas Blue

Ideal for all general sewing applications, they are standard length, ie 1″ (26 x .67mm).

Dorcas Red

Ideal for all general sewing but especially suitable for fine materials, 1 3/16″ (30 x .60mm). These pins are longer and finer than Dorcas Blue Box.

Dorcas Orange

Suitable for all sewing. Ideal for the dressmaker who prefers a longer pin, ie 1⅜″ (34 x .60mm).

Dorcas Glass-Headed Pins

Ideal for use in all craftwork, dressmaking etc. The larger head enables easier manipulation and has the advantage that the pins can always be seen. The glass-head, because it will not melt, allows garments to be pressed without causing damage.

Dorcas Ball-Point Pin

For use with knitted jersey-type fabrics, the ball-point parts rather than pierces the fabric.

Dorcas Foam Cushion-Top Box

Dorcas foam top box contains the longer and finer pins packed in the red box. The foam top makes a handy pincushion.

Royale Wedding Dress and Lace Pins

Especially designed for fine and light-coloured fabrics, these stainless steel pins will not mark and will not rust. They are suitable for making ''Special Occasion'' garments.

Diaden Lace Pins, Yellow Finish

Are made of brass and are specially designed for lace making. They are not recommended for dressmaking.

Adamantine Pins (Household)

A general purpose pin, suitable for both the home and the office; made in nickel-plated mild steel, they are not recommended for dress-making as they are too thick and they bend.

London Colour-Headed Pins

A general purpose pin with the advantage of the large coloured head which enables easier manipulation and has the advantage that the pins can be seen. These are manufactured in nickel-plated mild steel and they are extra-long. 1⅜″ (34 x .60mm). Ideal for craft.